THE QUOTABLE SLAYER

THE QUOTABLE SLAYER

Compiled by Micol Ostow
and Steven Brezenoff

Based on the hit television series
by Joss Whedon

POCKET BOOKS
NEW YORK   LONDON   TORONTO   SYDNEY

The following quotes were taken from the final shooting scripts for
each episode. The scripts may include words or even full dialogue
exchanges that were not in the final broadcast version of the show
because they were cut due to length. The quotes have been
verified against the aired version, but mistakes happen.
(A vague disclaimer's no one's friend. . . .)

First Pocket Books edition December 2003

POCKET BOOKS
An imprint of Simon & Schuster
Africa House
64–78 Kingsway
London
WC2B 6AH
www.simonsays.co.uk

Designed by Sammy Yuen Jr. (text and plate section)
and Berni Stevens (borders and b/w photo pages)
The text of this book was set in Times.
Printed in Great Britain by
William Clowes, Beccles, Suffolk
2 4 6 8 10 9 7 5 3 1
A CIP catalogue record for this book is available from
the British Library
ISBN 0-7434-7797-9

Buffy the Vampire Slayer™

To all the Buffy-philes out there
who are as rabid as we are!

*Micol would like to thank Steve Brezenoff for his
collaboration, Debbie Olshan at Fox for the guided
tour of the Buffyverse (and countless other favors),
Lisa Gribbin for picking up the torch, and
Lisa Clancy for letting me scribble all over the
Sunnydale High Yearbook.*

*Steve would like to thank Micol for the leg up, Lisa C.
and Lisa G. for advice and help along the way, and
the cast and crew of the best show ever for making my
Tuesday night every week for seven years.*

QUOTABLE INTRO

Buffy: "Careful. You're starting to talk like me."
Principal Wood: "I can think of worse people to
          emulate."

—"Storyteller"

It can be—and in fact *has* been—argued that *Buffy the Vampire Slayer* will go down in pop-culture history as a television show that subverted conventions, crossed genres, and redefined gender roles, raising the bar for the next wave of programming. Though the title suggests an easily dismissed concept, those who tuned in were instantly drawn to rich, complex characters, an organic mythology, and some of the sharpest, savviest, and most unique TV writing around. The fabrication of new words, the reappropriation of existing ones, and a complete disregard for conventional usage are hallmarks of *Buffy,* and the show's eminently quotable language has spawned a cult following fluent in *Buffy*-speak.

To that end, we've compiled in this book some of our best-loved quotes from the superheroine *Entertainment Weekly* dubbed "wittily literate." While certain categories need no explanation—*The Quotable Slayer* is just that: quotes by or about the Buffster that define her persona—others may seem more tenuous. "*Buffy* on . . . Slaying," for instance, focuses on the rules, regulations, and general state of being particular to she who hangs out a lot in cemeteries, while "*Buffy* on . . . War" highlights quotes on or about battle in a more global sense. And we've found on *Buffy* a vast distinction between sex and dating, and love. On *Buffy,* nuances are often subtle but rarely insignificant.

It would be impossible to include every fan's favourite quote within this compilation; frankly, there are far too many quotes—a surprising number of which defy categorization—and too many devout viewers to reconcile personal taste. We've made every effort to be exhaustive; we've even included a section at the end for miscellaneous quotes that we couldn't bear to cut. Ultimately people are bound to have personal favourites, but we hope that they will be satisfied (or even pleased!) with our endeavours. We're eminently grateful for the opportunity to have worked on what we hope will become an indispensable reference for the true Buffy-phile, but it goes without saying that the last word, of course, is the Slayer's.

Enjoy!

—Micol Ostow and Steven Brezenoff

THE QUOTABLE SLAYER

Quotable Slayer - Buffy

QUOTABLE SLAYER

"Destructo-Girl, that's me."

—Buffy, "The Witch"

"I don't think we've been properly introduced. I'm Buffy, and you are—" (plunges her stake into the vampire's heart) "—history."

—Buffy, "Never Kill a Boy on the First Date"

"If the apocalypse comes, beep me."

—Buffy, "Never Kill a Boy on the First Date"

Buffy: "I wasn't gonna use violence. I don't always use violence. Do I?"

Xander: "The important thing is, **you** believe that."

—"Inca Mummy Girl"

Buffy: "There was a cat. A cat here and then there was, another cat. And they fought, the cats, and then they left."

Ford: "Oh. I thought you were just slaying a vampire."

Buffy: "What? Whatting a what?"

—**"Lie to Me"**

Buffy: "It's just, like, nothing's simple. I'm always trying to work it out. Who to hate, or love . . . who to trust. . . . It's like the more I know, the more confused I get."

Giles: "I believe that's called growing up."

Buffy: (little voice) "I'd like to stop, then. Okay?"

—**"Lie to Me"**

Willow: "You're not even a teensy weensy bit curious about what kind of career you could have had? I mean, if you weren't already the Slayer and all."

Buffy: "Do the words 'sealed' and 'fate' ring any bells for you, Will? Why go there? I'm sorry . . . It's just—unless hell freezes over and every vamp in Sunnydale puts in for early retirement—I'd say my future is pretty much a non-issue."

—**"What's My Line? Part One"**

Buffy: "This career business has me contemplating the el weirdo that I am. Let's face it— instead of a job, I have a *calling*. Okay? No chess club or football games for me. I spend my free time in graveyards and dark alleys . . .

Angel: "Is that what you want? Football games?"

Buffy: "Maybe. Maybe not. But, you know what? I'm never going to get the chance to find out. I'm stuck with this deal."

—**"What's My Line? Part One"**

"She's the gnat in my ear. The gristle in my teeth. The bloody thorn in my *bloody* side!"

—**How does Spike love Buffy?**
"What's My Line? Part One"

Buffy: "Anybody besides Larry fit the werewolf profile?"

Willow: "There is one name that keeps getting spit out. Aggressive behavior, run-ins with authority, about a screenful of violent incidents . . ."

Buffy: "Okay, most of those weren't my fault."

—**"Phases"**

"I don't want any trouble. I just want to be alone and quiet, you know, with a chair, a fireplace, and a tea cozy. I'm not even sure what a tea cozy is, but I want one. Instead, I get trouble. Which I am willing to share."

—Buffy, "Anne"

"I'm Buffy. The vampire slayer. And you are . . . ?"
—Buffy reclaims her identity, "Anne"

Joyce: "I just wish you didn't have to be so secretive about things. I mean, it's not your fault you have a special circumstance. They should make allowances for you."

Buffy: "Mom. Please. I'm a Slayer. It's not like I have to ride the little bus to school."

—"Dead Man's Party"

"I thought, Homecoming Queen, I could open up a yearbook someday and say, 'I was there, I went to high school and had friends and for just one minute, I got to live in the world.' And there'd be proof. Proof that I was chosen for something other than this. Besides . . ." (pumping a shell into a gun) "I look cute in a tiara."

—Buffy, "Homecoming"

"Whoa, Summers, you drive like a spazz."
—Principal Snyder, "Band Candy"

Willow: "Speaking of people and things they do that are not like usual, anyone notice Buffy acting sort of different?"

Xander: "Let's see . . . killing zombies, torching sewer monsters, freeing the enslaved populace of a parallel dimension . . . nope. She's pretty much the same old Buffster."

—"Revelations"

Buffy: "What if I have lost my powers, Angel? I mean, for good?"

Angel: "You lived a long time without them. You can do it again."

Buffy: "I guess. . . . But what if I can't? I've seen too much now. I *know* what goes bump in the night. Not being able to fight it—what if I just hide under my bed, scared and helpless. . . . Or what if I just get pathetic? Hanging out at 'The Old Slayers' Home'— talking people's ears off about my glory days. . . . Showing them Mr. Pointy, the stake I had bronzed. . . ."

—"Helpless"

"I am way off my game, my game's left the country, it's in Cuernavaca."

—Buffy, re: the Cruciamentum, "Helpless"

"Before I became the Slayer I was . . . well, I don't want to say shallow, but . . . let's just say a certain person who shall remain nameless, let's call her 'Spordelia,' looked like a classical philosopher next to me."

—Buffy, "Helpless"

"Most of us never found the time to get to know you. But that doesn't mean we haven't noticed you. We don't talk about it much, but it's no secret that Sunnydale High isn't really like other schools. A lot of weird stuff happens here. . . . But whenever there was a problem or something creepy happened, you seemed to show up and stop it. Most of the people here have been saved by you . . . or helped by you . . . at one time or another. We're proud to say that the class of '99 has the lowest mortality rate of any graduating class in Sunnydale history. And we know at least part of that is because of you. So the senior class offers its thanks, and gives you this. It's from all of us, and it's got written here, 'Buffy Summers. Class Protector.'"

—Jonathan gives Buffy her due props, "Choices"

"Buffy, I've been through some fairly dark times in my life. Faced some scary things, among them the kitchen of the fabulous 'Ladies Night' club. Let me tell you something. When it's dark and I'm all alone, and I'm scared or freaking out or whatever, I always think, 'What would Buffy do?' . . . You're my hero."

—Xander, "The Freshman"

"Buffy would never just take off. It's just not in her nature, except that one time she disappeared for several months and changed her name."

—Willow boils it down, "The Freshman"

Buffy: "To me, a lot of the time, it feels like stuff's coming at me, you know, and I'm reacting as fast as I can, just trying to keep going. Just—just trying to be on my feet before the next thing hits."

Parker: "That sounds exhausting."

Buffy: "It really is."

—"The Harsh Light of Day"

Riley: "There's definitely something off about [Buffy]."

Graham: "Maybe she's Canadian."

—"The Initiative"

"[Buffy]'s all right, I guess. She's just kind of, I dunno . . . peculiar."

—Riley, "The Initiative"

Vamp: "Why don't you just go back where you came from? Things were great before you came. We ruled this campus. You ruined everything."

Buffy: "And they say one person can't make a difference."

—"Pangs"

"I'm the Slayer. . . . Slay-er. Chosen one? She who hangs out a lot in cemeteries . . . ? 'In every genera—' You know. I really don't feel like doing the routine. Ask around. Look it up: 'Slayer comma The.'"

—Buffy to Riley, "Doomed"

"She's cool. She's hot. She's tepid. She's all-temperature Buffy."

—Forrest, "Doomed"

Riley: "No weapons. No backup. You don't go after a demon that size by yourself."

Buffy: "I do."

—"Doomed"

Buffy: "Death. Pain. Apocalypse—none of them fun. Do you know what the Hellmouth is? Do they have a fancy term for it? 'Cause I went to high school on top of it. For three years. We *don't* have that much in common. This is a job to you."

Riley: "It's not just a job—"

Buffy: "It's an adventure, great, but for me it's destiny."

—"Doomed"

"I walk. I talk. I shop, I sneeze, I'm gonna be a fireman when the floods roll back. There's trees in the desert since you moved out, and I don't sleep on a bed of bones."
—Buffy's Dada-ist declaration of independence (to the First Slayer), "Restless"

"You think you know. What's to come, what you are . . . You haven't even begun."
—Tara (as the First Slayer) to Buffy, "Restless"

"I tell you I have this theory? It goes where, *you're* the one who's not *my* sister 'cause Mom adopted you from a shoebox full of baby howler monkeys, and never told you 'cause it could hurt your delicate baby feelings. Explains your fashion sense and smell."
—Dawn, "No Place Like Home"

Ben: "The Slayer? I don't know any Slayer."
Jinx: "Oh, I believe you do, sir. She's short, symmetrical, hair on top. Buffy something. . . ."
—"Checkpoint"

"I can beat up demons until the cows come home, and then I can beat up the cows."
—Buffy, "Intervention"

Willow: "What? What did [Buffy] do?"

Tara: "Everyone, before you jump all over her, people do strange things when someone they love dies. When I lost my mother I did some pretty dumb stuff, lying to my folks and staying out all night. . . .

Xander: "Buffy's boinking Spike."

Willow: "Oh. Well, Tara's right. Grief can be powerful and we shouldn't judge—"

Tara: "What are you, kidding? She's nuts!"

—**"Intervention"**

"Strength, and resilience—those are like words for hardness. I'm starting to feel like, like being the Slayer is sort of turning me to stone."

—**Buffy, "Intervention"**

"You did what was necessary—what I've always admired: being able to place your heart above all else. . . . I'm so proud of you. How far you've come. You're everything a Watcher—everything I could have hoped for."

—**Giles, "Spiral"**

Giles:	"Willow told me, but I didn't really let myself believe . . ."
Buffy:	"I take some getting used to. *I'm* still getting used to me."
Giles:	"It's . . . you're a . . ."
Buffy:	"A miracle?"
Giles:	"Yes. But then, I've always thought so."

> **—Re: Buffy's second coming, "Flooded"**

"I think I know why Joan's the boss. I'm like a superhero or something."

> **—Joan the Vampire Slayer kicks ass,**
> **"Tabula Rasa"**

Buffy:	"You know, when I got Xander's message that I was . . . fading away . . . I was . . . I mean, I actually got scared."
Willow:	"Well, sure. Who wouldn't?"
Buffy:	"Me. I wouldn't. Not too long ago. I probably would've welcomed it. But when he told me . . . I realized . . . Not saying I'm doing backflips about my life, but . . . I didn't . . . I mean, I don't . . . want to die. (looks at Willow) That's something, right?"

> **—"Gone"**

Buffy: "What, like I'm one of those losers who can't make friends outside her tight little circle? No, I'm very friendly, we bonded right away. Peas in a pod. Bonded peas."

Anya: "Really. What's Sophie's last name?"

Buffy: "Okay, shut up."

—**How to win friends and influence people, "Older and Far Away"**

Riley: "Got big stories to tell you too. We get half a sec, we can compare and contrast."

Buffy: "Did you die?"

Riley: "No."

Buffy: "I'm gonna win."

—**Catching up, "As You Were"**

Sam: "I've got to tell you, Buffy. I'm a little intimidated. I mean, patrolling with the real-live Slayer. . . . You're like . . . Santa Claus or the Buddha or something."

Buffy: "Fat and jolly?"

—**"As You Were"**

"You're still the first woman I ever loved and the strongest woman I ever knew. And I'm not advertising this to the missus, but still quite the hottie."

—**Riley, "As You Were"**

"Some type of . . . supergirl. Chosen to fight demons and save the world . . . ? That's ridiculous."

—Buffy, contemplating the el weirdo that is her life, "Normal Again"

"[Buffy's] a sweet girl, Spike, but hey, *issues*. And no wonder, with the coming back from the grave and whatnot. I had this cousin, got resurrected by some kooky shaman—whoo-boy! Was that a mess!"

—Clem does the guy-talk thing, "Seeing Red"

"Those kids got damn lucky, having a Slayer and a friend on campus there for 'em. Hope they appreciate it. . . . I know I did."

—Xander misses the halcyon days of high school, "Beneath You"

Buffy: "This week is going to be my first time really talking to kids. What if their problems are all weird and tricky? What if I can't help them?"

Xander: "I think you underestimate your familiarity with the world of weird and tricky."

—"Help"

Andrew: "So, how long have you followed Buffy?"
Xander: "I don't 'follow' her. She's my best friend."
Andrew: "Huh. . . . She seems like a good leader. Her
hair is shiny. . . . Does she make you stab
things?"

—"Bring on the Night"

"Let me tell you something about Buffy. I've been
through more battles with Buffy than you can
imagine. She's stopped everything that's ever come
against her. She's laid down her life—literally—to
protect the people around her. This girl has died, two
times, and she's still standing. You doubt her
motives, then you take the little bus to battle. I've
seen her heart—this time **not** literally—and I'll tell
you right now she cares more about your lives than
you will ever know. You gotta trust her. She's
earned it."

**—Xander lays it down for the potentials,
"Dirty Girls"**

"I've been alive a bit longer than you, and dead a lot longer than that. I've seen things you couldn't imagine, and done things I'd prefer you didn't. I don't exactly have a reputation for being a thinker; I follow my blood, which does not always rush in the direction of my head. So I've made a lot of mistakes. A lot of wrong bloody calls. A hundred plus years, only one thing I've ever been sure of. You. I'm not asking you for anything. When I tell you that I love you, it's not because I want you, or 'cause I can't have you—it has nothing to do with me. I love what you are, what you do, how you try. . . . I've seen your strength, and your kindness, I've seen the best and the worst of you and I understand with perfect clarity exactly what you are. You are a hell of a woman. You're the one, Buffy."

—Spike, "Touched"

Dawn: "And the Master grabbed Buffy from behind and **bit** her, she tried to move but he was too strong, he fed on her blood and he tossed her in the water, cackling insanely as the bubbles rose around her and she slowly **drowned** to death."

Vi: (upset) "Do you have any **other** stories?"

Dawn: "She gets up again, it's very romantic. Guys, you gotta stop worrying. It's Buffy. She always saves the day."

—"Chosen"

Quotable Watcher - Giles

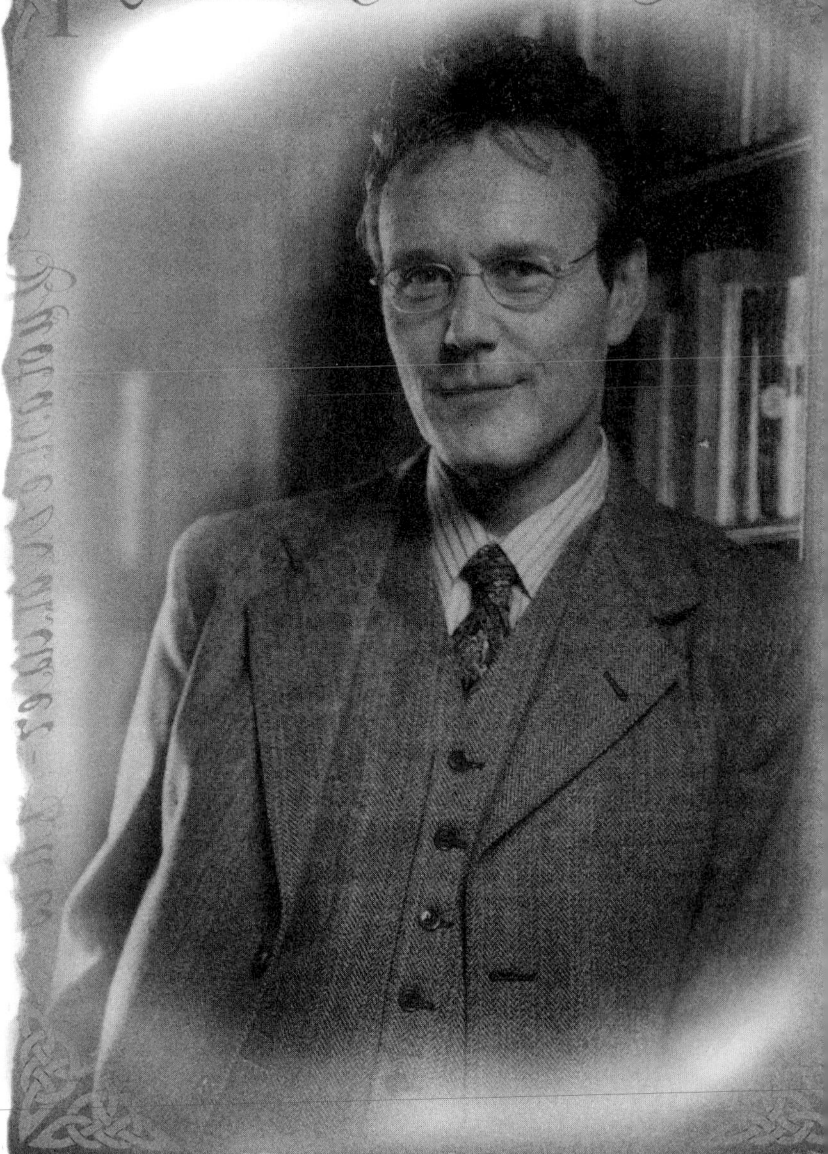

QUOTABLE WATCHER

"The vid library. I know it's not books, but it's still dark and musty; you'll be right at home."
                    —Buffy, to Giles, "Teacher's Pet"

Giles: "I have to stay and clean up. I'll be back in the Middle Ages."

Jenny: "Did you ever leave?"
                    —"I Robot, You Jane"

"He thought it would behoove me to have more contact with the students. I tried to explain that my vocational choice of librarian was a deliberate attempt to minimize said contact."

—Giles, re: involvement in the annual talentless show, "The Puppet Show"

Giles: "Grave robbing. Well, that's new. Interesting."

Buffy: "I know you meant to say 'gross and disturbing.'"

—"Some Assembly Required"

Buffy: "'Slaying entails certain sacrifices blah blah blah-bity blah I'm so stuffy give me a scone.'"

Giles: (witheringly) "It's like you **know** me."

—"Inca Mummy Girl"

Buffy: "You know, Giles, you're scaring me now. You need to have some fun. There's this amazing place you can go and sit down in the dark—and there are these moving pictures. And the pictures tell a *story*—"

Giles: "Ha, ha. Very droll. I'll have you know I have many relaxing hobbies."

Buffy: "Such as?"

Giles: "I'm very fond of cross-referencing."

Buffy: "Do you stuff your own shirts or do you send them out?"

—"Halloween"

Giles: "It's terribly simple. The good guys are stalwart and true. The bad guys are easily distinguished by their pointy horns or black hats and we always defeat them and save the day. Nobody ever dies . . . and everyone lives happily ever after."

Buffy: (with weary affection) "Liar."

    —Giles offers cold comfort, "Lie to Me"

Jenny: "Did anyone ever tell you you're kind of a fuddy duddy?"

Giles: "Nobody ever seems to tell me anything else."

Jenny: "Did anyone ever tell you you're kind of a sexy fuddy duddy?"

Giles: "That part usually gets left out. I can't imagine why."

    —"The Dark Age"

Xander: "Giles lived for school. He's still bitter there were only twelve grades."

Buffy: "He probably sat in math class thinking, 'There should be more math! This could be mathier!'"

    —"The Dark Age"

Buffy: "I'm worried about Giles. He was supposed to meet me here."

Angel: "Maybe he's late."

Buffy: "Giles? Who counts tardiness as the eighth deadly sin?"

—**"The Dark Age"**

Xander: "I knew this would happen. Nobody can be wound as straight and narrow as Giles without a dark side erupting. My Uncle Roary was the stodgiest taxidermist you ever met—by day—by night it was booze and whores and fur flying. . . . Were there any whores?"

Buffy: "He was alone."

Xander: "Give it time."

—**"The Dark Age"**

Giles: "I've been indexing the Watcher Diaries covering the past two centuries. You'd be amazed at how pompous and long-winded some of those Watchers were."

Buffy: "Color me stunned."

—**"What's My Line? Part One"**

Willow: "Are you mad at me?"

Giles: "Of course not. If I were angry I believe I would be making a strange clucking sound with my tongue."

—**"Faith, Hope & Trick"**

Buffy: "Faith, this is Giles."

Faith: "I seen him. If I'd a known they came this young and cute I'd've requested a transfer."

Buffy: "Okay, raise your hand if 'ew.'"

—**"Faith, Hope & Trick"**

Giles: "Right then. Good to see you. No need to panic."

Oz: "Just a thought? Poker. Not your game."

—**"Beauty and the Beasts"**

Willow: "It'll be okay when we get to Giles."

Oz: "Of course. I mean, even if he's sixteen, he's still Giles. Probably a pretty together guy."

Willow: "Yeah, well."

Oz: "What?"

Buffy: "Giles at sixteen. Less 'together guy,' more 'bad magic, hates the world, ticking time bomb guy.'"

—**On disturbing second childhoods,
"Band Candy"**

"You are so cool. You're like Burt Reynolds."

—**Joyce, "Band Candy"**

"God, you really were the little youthful offender, weren't you?"

—**Cordelia sees the Watcher's wild side,
"Gingerbread"**

Buffy: "Giles, you planning to step in with an explanation anytime soon?"

Giles: "Well, something . . . something very strange is happening."

Xander: "Can you believe the Watchers Council let this guy go?"

—**"Doppelgangland"**

Buffy: "You run?"

Giles: "And jump. And bend. And, occasionally, frolic."

Buffy: "Okay . . . And what's with *Motorbike and Scooter* magazine?"

Giles: "Congratulations. You've found me out: I'm a mod jogger."

—**On extracurricular hobbies, "The Freshman"**

Buffy: "Kathy, Giles. Giles, Kathy."

Willow: "He's our grown-up friend. But not in a creepy way."

—**A proper introduction, "Living Conditions"**

Giles: "I can't believe you served Buffy that beer."

Xander: "I didn't know it was evil!"

Giles: "You knew it was **beer**."

Xander: "Well, excuse me, Mr. I-spent-the-60s-in-an-electric-Kool-Aid-funky-satan-groove."

—**"Beer Bad"**

Giles:	"I'm quite 'with it' when it comes to music—and I have the record albums to prove it."
Buffy:	"But it's your cutting-edge eight-tracks that keep you ahead of the scene."

—**"Wild at Heart"**

Giles:	"Angel, I'm glad you're looking out for her. But I feel I have to remind you, she's not helpless and it's not your job to keep her safe."
Angel:	"It's not yours anymore either. Are **you** going to walk away?"

—**"Pangs"**

Buffy:	"Giles, the sarcasm accomplishes nothing."
Giles:	"Well, it was sort of an end in itself."

—**"Pangs"**

Buffy:	"We don't say 'Indian.'"
Giles:	"Yes! Right. Always behind on the terms. Still trying not to refer to you lot as 'bloody colonials.'"

—**"Pangs"**

Olivia: "All that time you used to talk about witchcraft and darkness and the like . . . I just thought you were pretentious."

Giles: "Oh, I was. But I was also right."

Olivia: "So everything you told me was true."

Giles: "Well, no. I wasn't actually one of the original members of Pink Floyd."

—**"Hush"**

Spike: "Giles? Why the hell are you suddenly a Fyarl demon? 'Cause I like to think I'm pretty observant, and I never saw a sign of it, I swear."

Giles: "It's a funny story. If funny meant horrific."

—**"A New Man"**

Buffy: "I just wish I knew what I needed. I keep thinking, let's ask Giles, and then I remember."

Xander: "He'd be great right now. He'd find himself in a second. Nobody's cooler in a crisis."

—**"A New Man"**

Giles: "It's a meeting of grown-ups. It couldn't possibly be of interest to you lot."

Willow: "You have grown-up friends?"

—**"Where the Wild Things Are"**

Xander: "Oh. Okay. You and Willow go do the superpower thing. I'll stay behind and putter around the batcave [indicates Giles] with crusty old Alfred here."

Giles: "Ahh. I am no Alfred, sir. You forget— Alfred had a **job**."

—**"The Yoko Factor"**

"I'm great with the pacing and the saying of 'hmmmm,' and 'ahhhhh,' and 'Good Lord!' "

—**Giles, "The Yoko Factor"**

Tara: "What's so bad about them coming here? Aren't they good guys? I mean, Watchers, that's just like a whole buncha other Gileses, right?"

Buffy: "Yes! They're scary and horrible!"

—**Re: the hairy eyeball, "Checkpoint"**

Buffy: "A guide, but no water or food. So it leads me to the sacred place and then a week later it leads you to my bleached bones?"

Giles: "Buffy, really. It takes more than a week to bleach bones."

—**"Intervention"**

Spike: "You don't suppose . . . you and I . . . we're not related, are we?"

Anya: "There is a ruggedly handsome resemblance."

Giles: (dismayed) "And you do inspire a particular feeling of familiarity . . . and disappointment. (weakly, re: himself) Older brother?"

Spike: "Father! (glares) My god how I must hate you."

—Losing memory and reassigning identity, "Tabula Rasa"

Willow: "Is there anything you don't know everything about?"

Giles: "Synchronized swimming. Complete mystery to me."

—"Lessons"

"In the end, we are all who we are, no matter how much we may appear to have changed."

—Giles to Buffy, "Lessons"

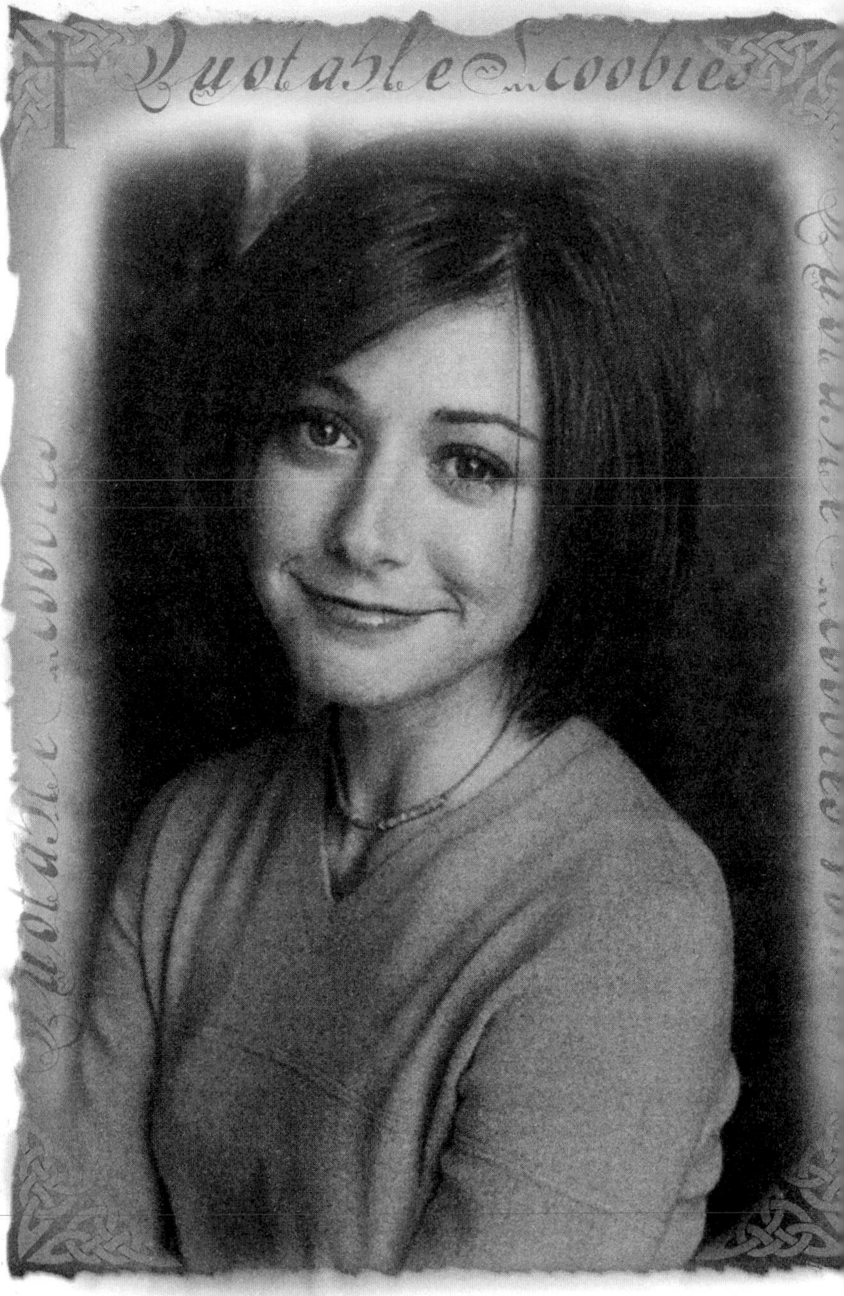
Quotable Scoobies

QUOTABLE SCOOBIES

*"**This** is the crack team that foils my every plan? I am deeply shamed."*
—Spike, "Something Blue"

WILLOW

"Oh boy, time for geometry. (off Xander and Buffy's looks) It's fun if you make it fun."

—Willow, "Angel"

"It could be anyone. It could be me. . . . It's not, though."
—Willow explaining why human criminals are more upsetting, "The Puppet Show"

Willow: "What could a demon possibly want from me?"

Xander: "What's the square root of eight hundred forty-one?"

Willow: "Twenty-nine. Oh, yeah."

—**"The Puppet Show"**

Willow: "Even I was bored. And I'm a science nerd."

Buffy: "Don't say that."

Willow: "I'm not ashamed. It's the computer age; nerds are in. . . . They're still in, right?"

—**"Prophecy Girl"**

"I'm probably the only girl in school who has the Coroner's Office bookmarked as a 'favorite place.'"

—**Willow, "Some Assembly Required"**

Angel: "I guess I need help. And you're the first person I thought of."

Willow: "Help? You mean like on homework? No, 'cause you're old and you already know stuff."

Angel: "I want you to track someone down. On the Net."

Willow: "Oh! Great. I'm **so** the Net girl."

—**"Lie to Me"**

Giles: "Don't warn the tadpoles?"

Willow: "I—I have frog fear."

—**"What's My Line? Part One"**

Willow: "Great! I'll call Xander, ask him to join us. What's his number? Oh, yeah: 1-800-I'm-Dating-a-Skanky-Ho."

Buffy: "Me-ow!"

Willow: "Really? Thanks! I've never gotten a 'me-ow' before."

—**"Phases"**

"That's right, big boy. . . . Come and get it."

—**Willow to vampire, "Anne"**

Willow: "I understand you having to bail and I can forgive that. I have to make allowances for what you're going through and just be a grown-up about it."

Buffy: "You're loving this moral superiority thing."

Willow: "It's like a drug."

—**"Dead Man's Party"**

Mrs. Rosenberg: "Willow, you cut off your hair! That's a new look."

Willow: "Yeah, it's just a sudden whim that I had . . . in August."

—**A conversation in January, "Gingerbread"**

"Mom, I'm not an age group. I'm me. Willow group. It's probably hard to accept, but I can do stuff. Nothing bad or dangerous. But I can do spells. Hear this, Ma! I'm a rebel! I'm having a rebellion! I'm not acting out—I'm a WITCH. I make pencils float. I summon the four elements! Well—two elements—but four soon! And I'm dating a musician!"

—Willow, "Gingerbread"

"Bored now."

—Vampwillow, "Doppelgangland"

Giles: "[Willow] was . . . truly the finest of all of us."

Xander: "Way better than me."

Giles: "Much, much better."

**—A fitting—though premature—
eulogy, "Doppelgangland"**

"That's me as a vampire? I'm so evil . . . and skanky. And I think I'm kinda gay."

**—Willow on encountering her
dark side, "Doppelgangland"**

Willow: "The coroner's office said she was missing an ear. So, I'm thinking maybe we're looking for a witch. There are some great spells that work much better with an ear in the mix."

Buffy: "That's one fun little hobby you've got there."

—"Pangs"

"I happen to think mine is the level head and yours is the one that things would roll off of."

—Willow defending her judgment, "Pangs"

"[Willow] was just some egghead who tutored me a little in high school. She's nice, but please . . . captain of the nerd squad."

—Percy, not interested in dating Willow, "Doomed"

"You two are the two who are the two. I'm the other one."

—Willow to Buffy and Xander, feeling left out, "The Yoko Factor"

Dawn: "My nog tastes funny. I think I got one with rum in it."

Willow: "That's bad."

Xander: "Yeah, now Santa's gonna pass you right by, naughty boozehound."

Willow: "He always passes me by. Something always puts him off. Could be the big honkin' menorah."

—"The Body"

"I'm a big fan of school. You know me, I'm all, 'Go, school, it's your birthday!' Or something to that effect."

—Willow, "Tough Love"

Tara: "You've got . . . that's serious power."
Willow: "But it's good-witch power, not bad-witch power. You know, Glenda-in-a-bubble power, not Margaret Hamilton-on-a-bicycle power."

—"Tough Love"

Dawn: "How are you?"
Willow: "A little confused. I mean, I'm sweaty, I'm trapped, no memory, hiding in a pipe, from a vampire—I think I'm kind of gay."

—It's all coming back, "Tabula Rasa"

"When someone falls for Willow, they stay fallen."

—Buffy, "Normal Again"

"You made the decision to stop for a reason. You promised us. And can I just ask—what's with the makeover of the damned?"

—Xander, not loving Willow's new look, "Villains"

"Bored now."

—Willow, "Villains"

"I can't believe that was Willow. I mean, I've known her as long as you guys. Willow was . . . you know. She packed her own lunches and wore floods and she was always . . . just Willow."

—Has it been so long? Jonathan, "Two to Go"

"Let me tell you something about Willow: She's a loser. And she always has been. Everyone picked on Willow in junior high, high school, up until college with her stupid mousy ways and now—Willow's a junkie. . . . The only thing Willow was ever good for, the only thing going for me, were those moments— just moments—when Tara would look at me . . . and I was wonderful. And that will never happen again."

—Willow, "Two to Go"

Buffy: "Will, back off before somebody gets hurt."
Willow: "How about if I back off right after?"

—"Two to Go"

Willow: "When you brought me here, I thought it was to kill me. Or lock me in some mystical dungeon for all eternity, or with the torture . . . Instead you go all Dumbledore on me. I'm learning about magic. I'm all about energy and gaia and root systems."
Giles: "Do you want to be punished?"
Willow: "I wanna be Willow."

—"Lessons"

XANDER

"I am Xander, King of the Cretins, and all lesser cretins must bow before me."

—Xander, "The Witch"

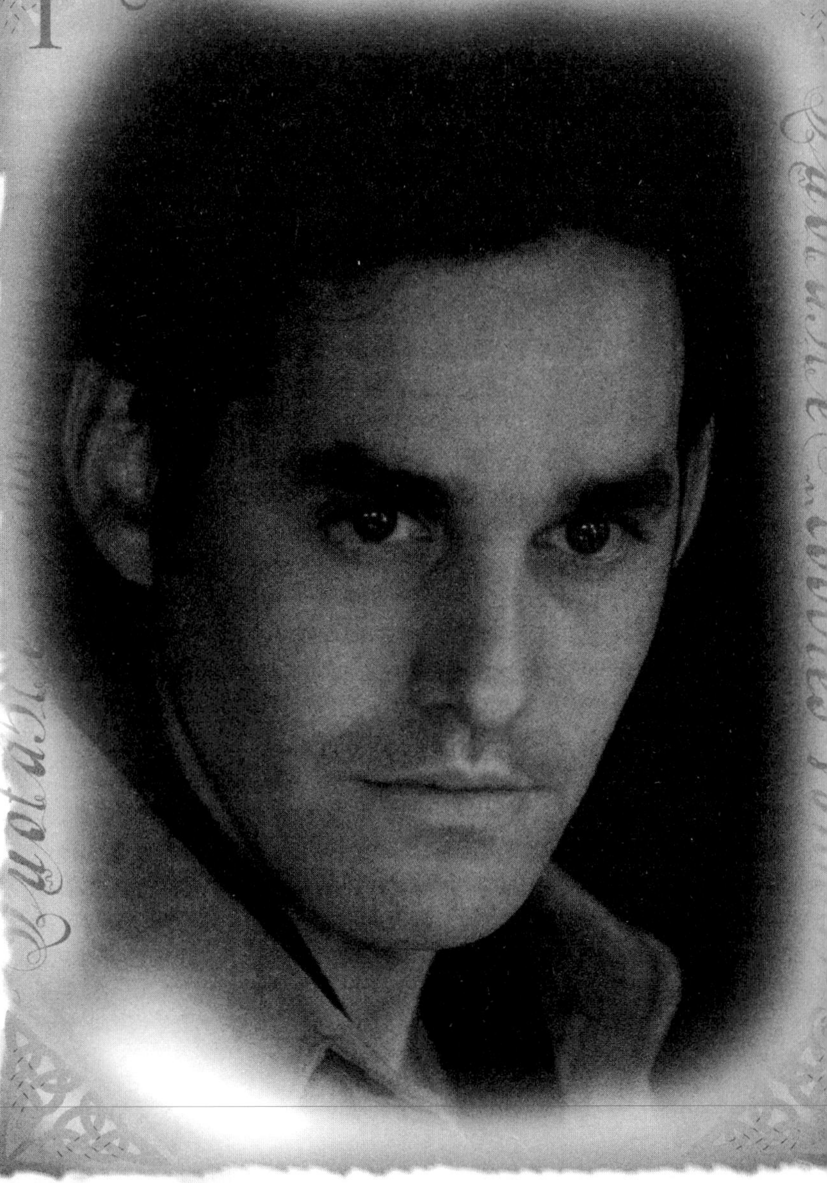

"I'd give anything to be able to turn invisible. I wouldn't be beating people up. I'd use my power to **protect** the girl's locker room."

> **—Xander, "Out of Mind, Out of Sight"**

"You know, Buffy, Spring Fling isn't just any dance. It's a time when the students all sort of choose a . . . a mate, and, and we can observe their mating ritual and tag them before they migrate. **Just kill me.**"

> **—Xander, brushing up on his dating skills, "Prophecy Girl"**

"I don't handle rejection well. Funny, considering how much practice I've had."

> **—Xander, "Prophecy Girl"**

"I don't get wild. Wild on me equals spazz."

> **—Xander, "Halloween"**

Buffy: "Xander, how do you feel about rifling through Giles's personal files, see if you can shed some light?"

Xander: "I feel pretty good about it. Does that make me a sociopath?"

> **—"The Dark Age"**

"So you're a slayer, huh? I like that in a woman."

> **—Xander has particular romantic inclinations, "What's My Line? Part Two"**

Buffy: "You and bug people, Xander. What's up with that?"

Xander: "But this dude was different than the praying mantis lady. He was a man *of* bugs. Not a man who *was* a bug."

—Re: the Tarakan bug-man assassin, "What's My Line? Part Two"

Xander: "I have a plan. We use me as bait."

Buffy: "You mean, make Angel come after **you**?"

Xander: "No, I mean chop me into little pieces and stick me on hooks for fish to nibble at, 'cause that would be more fun than my life."

—Glass half-empty, "Bewitched, Bothered, and Bewildered"

"I don't get this. The candy's supposed to make you all immature and stuff, but I ate a ton and I don't feel any diff—never mind."

—Xander, "Band Candy"

Jack: "What are you, retarded?"

Xander: "No! I mean I had to do that test when I was seven, a little slow in some stuff, mostly math and spacial relations, but certainly not 'challenged' or anything."

—"The Zeppo"

"Excuse me: who, at the crucial moment, distracted the lead demon by allowing her to pummel him about the head?"

—Xander, re: his battle strategy, "The Zeppo"

Giles: "Xander, I think it best if you keep to the rear of battle in the future. For your own sake."

Xander: "But gee, Mr. White, if Clark and Lois get all the big stories I'll never be a real reporter."

—"The Zeppo"

Xander: "You need a thing. One thing nobody else has. What do I have?"

Oz: "An exciting new obsession—which I feel makes you very special."

—"The Zeppo"

Xander: "You girls need a lift?"
Buffy: "What is that?"
Xander: "What do you mean, what is it? It's my thing!"
Willow: "Your thing?"
Xander: "My **thing** . . ."
Buffy: "Is this a penis metaphor?"

—Wheels are key to cool, "The Zeppo"

Willow: "He's still doing his cross-country see-America thing. He said he wasn't coming back until he'd driven to all fifty states."

Buffy: "Did you explain about Hawaii?"

Willow: "Well, he seemed so determined."

—**"The Freshman"**

Oz: "Xander's a civilian."

Josh: "Ohh. Townie, huh? Didn't know. He looked so normal."

—**A student of the open road, "Fear, Itself"**

Xander: "I happen to be very biteable, pal. I'm moist and delicious."

Spike: "All right, yeah fine. You're a nummy treat."

—**"Hush"**

Xander: "We're part of the team. [Buffy] needs us."

Spike: "Or you're just the same tenth-grade loser you've always been . . . and she's too much of a softy to cut you loose."

—**"Doomed"**

Xander: "I move pretty fast. You know, a man's always after . . ."

Joyce: "Conquest?"

Xander: "I'm a conquistador."

Joyce: "What about comfort?"

Xander: "I'm a comfortador, also."

—**"Restless"**

Spike: "Giles here is gonna teach me to be a Watcher. Says I got the stuff."

Giles: "Spike's like a son to me."

Xander: "Well, that's good. I was into that for a while, but I got other stuff going on. Gotta have something. Gotta be always moving forward."

Buffy: "Like a shark."

Xander: "A shark with feet. And much less . . . fins."

Spike: "And on **land**."

—**"Restless"**

Snyder: "Where you from, Harris?"

Xander: "Well, the basement, mostly."

—**"Restless"**

"You're a whipping boy, raised by mongrels and set on a sacrificial stone."

—**Principal Snyder to Xander, "Restless"**

"You know what? I'm sick of this crap. I'm sick of being the guy who eats the insects and gets the funny syphilis! As of this moment, it's *over*. I'm finished being everybody's butt monkey!"

> **—Xander re: being under Dracula's thrall, "Buffy vs. Dracula"**

Tara: "At least she didn't do too much damage."

Xander: "Are you kidding? Double-glazed glass is not cheap. Also, the jamb has to be completely rebuilt—Oh, dear god, I'm the grown-up who sees the world through my job. I'm my uncle Dave the plumber and I must be shunned."

Willow: "Okay."

> **—"I Was Made to Love You"**

"[Xander] doesn't travel well. He's like fine shrimp."

> **—Anya, "Spiral"**

Willow: "There were, you know, razor scooters and pictures of the Vulcan woman on *Enterprise*."

Xander: "Ooh! I mean, pff, nerds."

> **—The trio's lair is Xander's dream getaway, "Doublemeat Palace"**

"Man, a nerd goes into hiding, he really goes into hiding. Upside of spending all that time shoved inside a locker. . . . Not that I would know."
—Xander, "Older and Far Away"

Buffy: "They told me I was sick. Crazy, I guess. And that Sunnydale and . . . all of this, none of it was real. Just part of some delusion in my head."

Xander: "Come on! That's ridiculous! What, you think this isn't real just 'cause of all the vampires and the demons and the ex-vengeance demons and the sister that used to be a ball of universe-destroying energy . . . ? Well, I'm real."
—"Normal Again"

Buffy: "Someone was using [this camera] to spy on me. On the house. Xander thinks it might've been you."

Spike: "Oh, the great Xander thinks so! Shudder, gasp! It must be true!"
—"Entropy"

Xander: "I hurt you, so you get me back? Very mature."

Anya: "No, the mature solution is to spend your whole life telling stupid, pointless jokes so no one will notice you're just a scared, insecure little boy."

—**"Entropy"**

Anya: "None of this would be happening if it weren't for you."

Xander: "You think I don't know that? You think I'm the hero of this piece? I saw the gun. Before Warren even raised it, I saw it, and . . . I couldn't move. He shot two of my friends before I could even . . . You want me to know how useless I am? That it's my fault? Thanks. Already got the memo."

—**"Two to Go"**

"You're not the only one with powers, you know. You may be a hopped-up über-witch, but this carpenter can dry-wall you into the next century."

—**Xander to Willow, "Grave"**

Buffy: "I think I may have destroyed Dawn's social life in all of thirty seconds."

Xander: "Ah, being popular isn't that great, or so I've read in books."

—**"Lessons"**

"I forgot high school's unwritten rules of hallway etiquette. Of course, no one ever explained them to me; they'd just stuff me in a locker till I drew my own conclusions."

—Xander, "Beneath You"

Xander: "Anya and I are done. I love being single. I'm a strong, successful male who's giddy at the thought of all the women I will no doubt be dating in the near future."

Buffy: "Strong, successful males say 'giddy'?"

— "Selfless"

"If you die, I'll just bring you back to life. That's what I do."

—Xander to Buffy, natch, "End of Days"

"Party in my eye socket and everyone's invited!" (beat) "Sometimes I should just not say words."

—Xander, "Chosen"

ANGEL/ANGELUS

Buffy: "Who are you?"
Angel: "A friend."
Buffy: (exasperated) "Well, maybe I don't want a friend."
Angel: "I didn't say I was **yours**."

—"Welcome to the Hellmouth"

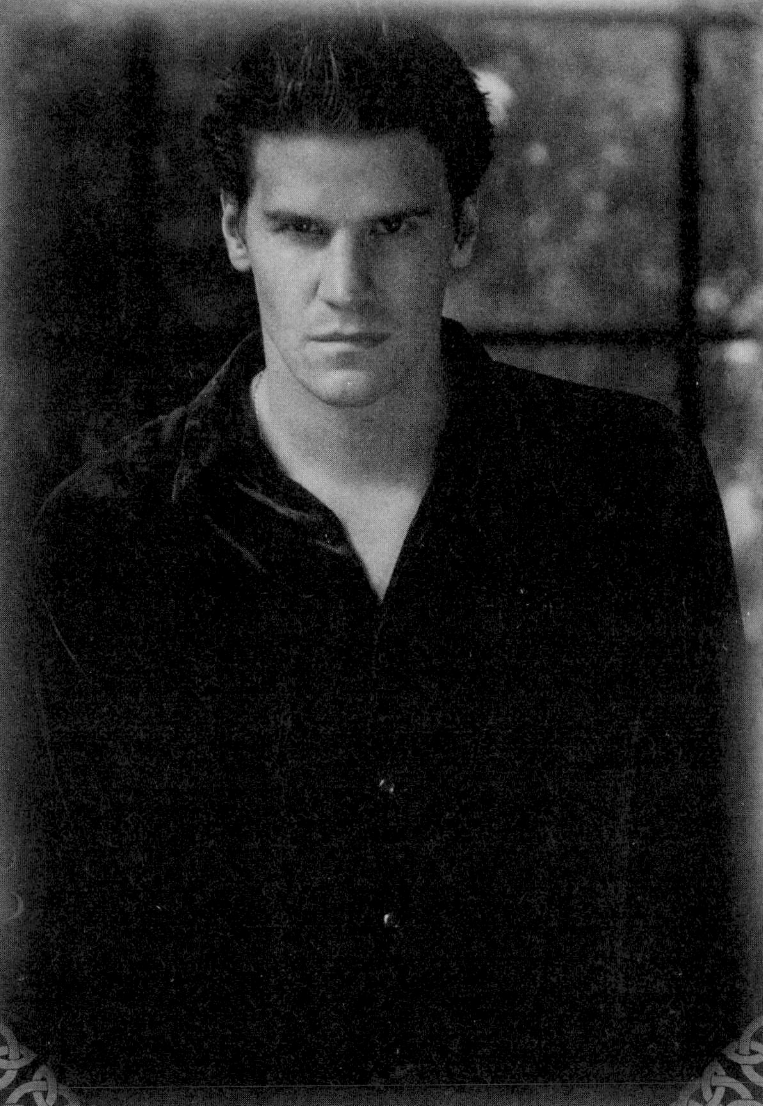

"Hel-lo, salty goodness."

> **—Cordelia, on seeing Angel for the first time,**
> **"Never Kill a Boy on the First Date"**

Buffy: "Well, what does your family think of your career choice?"

Angel: "They're dead."

> **—"Angel"**

"You and I both know the things you hunger for, the things you need. Hey, nothing to be ashamed of; it's who we are, it's what makes Eternal life worth living."

> **—Darla to Angel, "Angel"**

"Angel. He was the most vicious creature I ever met. I miss him."

> **—The Master, "Angel"**

Angel: "I'm just an animal, right?"

Buffy: "You're not an animal. Animals I like."

> **—"Angel"**

Angel: "This isn't some fairy tale: When I kiss you, you don't wake up from a deep sleep and live happily ever after."

Buffy: "No. When you kiss me, I want to die."

> **—"Reptile Boy"**

"Things used to be pretty simple. A hundred years just hanging out, feeling guilty. I really honed my brooding skills. Then she comes along . . ."

—**Angel re: Buffy, "Lie to Me"**

Buffy: "You knew that if the demon was in danger it would jump into the nearest dead guy."

Angel: "I put it in danger."

Willow: "And it jumped."

Angel: "But I've had a demon inside me for a couple hundred years just waiting for a good fight."

Buffy: "Winner and still champion."

—**"The Dark Age"**

"Angel—you're the one freaky thing in my freaky world that makes sense to me."

—**Buffy, "What's My Line? Part One"**

"Angel's our friend. Except I don't like him."

—**Xander, "What's My Line? Part Two"**

Angel: "You don't think about the future?"

Buffy: "No."

Angel: "How can you say that? You're not like me. You could have a normal life. You really don't care what happens a year from now? Five years from now . . . ?"

Buffy: "I-I *can't* care. Angel. When I try to look into the future, all I can see . . . is you—All I want is *you*."

Angel: "I know the feeling."

—"Bad Eggs"

"As long as there is injustice in this world . . . As long as scum like you is walking—or, well, rolling—the streets, I'll be around. Look over your shoulder. I'll be there."

—Angelus to Spike, "Innocence"

Spike: "You've really got a yen to hurt this girl, haven't you?"

Angelus: "She made me feel like a human being. That's not the kind of thing you just forgive."

—Angelus re: Buffy, "Innocence"

51

Cordelia: "Oh, my god! I invited [Angel] into my car once! That means he could come back into my car whenever he wants!"

Xander: "Yep. Now you're doomed to having to give him and his vamp pals a lift whenever they feel like it. And those guys never chip in for gas."

—**"Passion"**

"[Angel] saved me from a horrible flame-y death. That sort of makes me like him again."

—**Willow, "Revelations"**

Buffy: "We're not friends. Never were. I can fool Giles, I can fool my friends, but I can't fool myself. Or Spike, for some reason. What I want from you, I can never have. You don't need me to take care of you anymore, so I'm gonna go."

Angel: "I don't accept that."

Buffy: "You have to."

Angel: "There must be some way we can still see each other."

Buffy: "There is. Just tell me you don't love me."

—**"Lovers Walk"**

Angel: "I was a man once."

Jenny Calendar/The First: "Oh, yes. And what a man you were! A drunken, whoring layabout and a terrible disappointment to your parents."

Angel: "I was . . . young . . . I never had the chance to—"

Jenny Calendar/The First: "— to die of syphilis? You were a worthless being before you were ever a monster."

—**"Amends"**

Angel: "[The First] told me to kill you. It told me to take you, to lose my soul in you and become a monster again."

Buffy: "I know what it told you. Why does it matter?"

Angel: "Because I wanted to! Because I want you so badly, I want to take comfort in you and I know it'll cost me my soul and part of me doesn't care. I'm weak. I've never been anything else. It's not the demon in me that needs killing, Buffy. It's the man."

—**"Amends"**

Buffy: "Angel, I love you so much—and I've tried to make you go away; I **killed** you and it didn't help . . . and I hate it. I hate that it's so hard . . . that you can hurt me so much. . . . I know everything you've done because you did it to me. I wish I wished you dead. But I don't. I can't."

Angel: "Buffy, please . . . just this once . . . let me be strong."

Buffy: "Strong is fighting. It's hard and it's painful and it's every day. It's what we have to do and we can do it together, but if you're too much of a coward for that, then burn."

—"Amends"

"Time was, I thought humans existed just to hurt each other. But then I came here. And I found out that there were other kinds of people. People who genuinely wanted to do right. They still make mistakes. They fall down. But they keep trying. Keep caring."

—Angel to Faith, "Consequences"

"I know. What it's like, to take a life. To feel a future, a world of possibility—snuffed out by your own hand. I know the power in it. The exhilaration. It was like a drug for me."

—Also Angel to Faith, "Consequences"

"What kind of life can you offer [Buffy]? I don't see a lot of Sunday picnics in the offing. Skulking in the shadows, hiding from the sun—she's a blossoming young girl! You want to keep her from the life she should have till it's passed by her, and by God I think that's a little selfish. Is that what you came back from Hell for? Is that your greater purpose?"

—The Mayor to Angel, "Choices"

Parker: "Don't you hate guys that are all 'I'm dark and brooding so give me love'?"

Buffy: "I . . . I've never met that type."

—re: Angel, "The Harsh Light of Day"

"Well, there you go. Even when he's good he's all Mr. Billowy Coat King of Pain."

—Riley does the jealous thing re: Angel, "The Yoko Factor"

"You know, **I** started it. The whole . . . having a soul. Before it was all the 'cool new thing.'"

—Angel irked that everybody (read: Spike) is doing it, "Chosen"

CORDELIA

"I would kill to live in L.A. Being that close to that many shoes . . ."

—Cordelia, "Welcome to the Hellmouth"

"I'm just not the type to settle. If I go into a clothing store, I always have to have the most expensive thing, not because it's **expensive**, but because it **costs** more."

—Cordelia, "The Harvest"

"It was . . . let's just say I haven't been able to eat a thing since yesterday. . . . I think I lost like seven and a half ounces—way swifter than the so-called diet that quack put me on. Oh, I'm not saying we should kill a teacher every day so I can lose weight, I'm just saying when tragedy strikes we have to look on the bright side."

—Cordelia's glass half full, "Teacher's Pet"

"People who think their problems are so huge craze me. Like the time I sort of ran over this girl on her bike, and it was the most traumatizing event of my **life**, and she's trying to make it all about **her** leg! Like my pain meant **nothing** . . . !"

—Cordelia, "Out of Mind, Out of Sight"

"Oh, you should have seen [Mitch]—lying there, all black and blue. . . . How's he going to look in our prom pictures? How will I ever be able to show them to anyone?"

—**Cordelia, "Out of Mind, Out of Sight"**

"Thank you. For making the right choice. For showing how much you love me!"

—**Cordelia on being crowned May Queen, "Out of Mind, Out of Sight"**

Cordelia: "Somebody's after me! Someone just tried to kill Ms. Miller! She was helping me with homework! And Mitch and Harmony . . . ! This is all about me! Me! Me! Me!"

Xander: "Wow. For once she's right."

—**"Out of Mind, Out of Sight"**

"You think I'm never lonely, just 'cause I'm so cute and popular? I can be surrounded by people and be completely alone. It's not like any of them really know me. I don't even know if they really **like** me half the time. People just want to be in the popular zone. Sometimes when I talk, everyone's so busy agreeing with me, they don't hear a word I say."

—**Cordelia, "Out of Mind, Out of Sight"**

"It was a nightmare. A nightmare. [My parents] **promised** me we were going to St. Croix, and then at the last minute, they just **decide** we're gonna visit Tuscany instead. Art. Buildings. Totally beachless for a month and a half. No one has suffered as I have suffered. Of course, I think that kind of adversity builds character. But then I thought, well, I already **have** a lot of character. I mean, it is possible to have too much character, isn't it?"

> **—Cordelia, re: summer vacation plans gone bust, "When She Was Bad"**

Cordelia: "Devon, I know I told you I'd be at the dance tonight, but I'm not one of your little groupies. I won't be all doe-eyed, looking up at you, standing at the edge of the stage."

Devon: "Got it."

Cordelia: "So, I'll see you afterwards?"

Devon: "Sure. Where do you want to meet?"

Cordelia: "I'll be standing at the edge of the stage."

> **—Cordelia working the finer points of dating, "Inca Mummy Girl"**

"This exchange-student thing has been a horrible nightmare. They don't even speak American!"

> **—Cordelia, "Inca Mummy Girl"**

"Look, Buffy, you may be hot stuff when it comes to demonology or whatever, but when it comes to dating, I'm the Slayer."

—**Cordelia, "Halloween"**

"I aspire to help my fellow man. Check. I mean, as long as he's not, like, smelly or dirty or something gross."

—**Cordelia's accurate personality assessment, "What's My Line? Part One"**

Cordelia: "I can't even believe you. You drag me out of bed for a ride? What am I, mass transportation?"

Xander: "That's what a lot of the guys say. But it's just locker room talk. I never pay it any mind . . ."

Cordelia: "Great. So now I'm your taxi and your punching bag—"

Xander: "I like to think of you more as my witless foil—but have it your way. Come on, Cordy. You can't be a member of the Scooby Gang if you aren't willing to be inconvenienced now and then—"

Cordelia: "Oh, right. 'Cause I lie awake at night hoping you tweekos will be my best friends. And that my first husband will be a balding, demented, homeless man—"

—**"What's My Line? Part One"**

"You know what you are, Harmony? You're a sheep. All you ever do is what everyone else does, so you can say you did it first. And here I am scrambling for your approval, when I'm way cooler than you are because I'm not a sheep! I do what I want, I wear what I want, and you know what? I'll date whoever I want to date, no matter how lame he is!"

> **—Cordelia "defending" Xander, "Bewitched, Bothered, and Bewildered"**

"I'm the dip!"

> **—You have to admire the purity of it: Cordelia, "Dead Man's Party"**

Willow: "Maybe we shouldn't be too couple-y around Buffy."

Cordelia: "Oh, you mean 'cause of how the only guy that ever liked her turned into a vicious killer and had to be put down like a dog?"

Xander: "Can she cram complex issues into a nutshell, or what?"

> **—"Faith, Hope & Trick"**

61

Gorch: "I'm gonna —"

Cordelia: "I know, rip out my innards, boil my brain and eat it for brunch—now, listen up, needle-brain, Buffy and I have taken out four of your cronies, including your girlfriend. . . . Point is, I haven't even worked up a sweat. See, in the end, Buffy's good, but she's just the runner-up. *I'm the Queen.* If I get mad, what do you think I'm gonna do to you?"

—"Homecoming"

"Actually, I'm looking forward to [the SATs]. I do well on standardized tests." (off the Scoobies' looks.) "What? I can't have layers?"

—Cordelia, "Band Candy"

Wesley: "Was that vampire . . . ?"

Cordelia: "Willow. They got Willow. . . . So, you doing anything tonight?"

—In mourning, "Doppelgangland"

SPİKE

"I was actually at Woodstock. That was a weird gig. Fed off a flower person and spent six hours watching my hands move."

—Spike re: the questionable benefits of longevity, "School Hard"

"Oh yeah, I did a couple Slayers in my time. Don't like to brag. Oh, who am I kidding, I love to brag."
—**Spike, "School Hard"**

"I know you haven't been in the game for a while, mate, but we do still kill people. It's sort of our *raison d'être*, you know."
—**Spike to the newly re-evil Angelus, "Innocence"**

"Real love isn't brains, children, it's blood; it's blood screaming inside you to work its will. I may be love's bitch, but at least I'm man enough to admit it."
—**Spike, "Lovers Walk"**

"Now, that was fun. GOD! It's been so long since I had a decent spot of violence! Really puts things in perspective."
—**Spike, "Lovers Walk"**

Harmony: "You love that tunnel more than me."
Spike: "I love syphilis more than you."
—**"The Harsh Light of Day"**

"Spike had a little trip to the vet, and now he doesn't chase the other puppies anymore."
—**Spike on the chip, "Pangs"**

"Leave that one. He looks like he's ready to drop any minute, and I think I can eat someone if they're already dead."

    —Xander's syphilis meets Spike's chip, "Pangs"

Spike: "Bloody hell, woman! You're cutting off my circulation."

Buffy: "You don't have any circulation."

Spike: "Well, it pinches."

    —The ties that bind (literally), "Pangs"

"I came to you in friendship! Well, all right, seething hatred."

    —Spike, "Pangs"

Giles: "We can't let you go until we're sure you're impotent."

Spike: "Hey!"

Giles: "Sorry. Poor choice of words. Till we know you're . . ."

Buffy: "Flaccid?"

    —"Something Blue"

Buffy: "You know what? I think you don't *want* us to let you go. Maybe we made it too comfy here."

Spike: "Comfy? Do I look comfy? I'm chained in a bathtub drinking pig's blood from a novelty mug. Doesn't rate huge in the Zagat's guide."

—On elusive creature comforts, "Something Blue"

Xander: "You were trying to stake yourself!"

Spike: "Fag off. It's no concern of yours."

Xander: "Is too. For one thing, that's my shirt you're about to dust. And for another, we've shared a lot here. You should have trusted me enough to do it for you."

—"Doomed"

Buffy: "You ready?"

Xander: "Let's rock 'n' roll."

Spike: "'Let's rock 'n' roll'? You actually talk like that?"

—"Doomed"

"What's this? Just sitting about watching the telly when there's evil afoot?"

—Spike wants to get on with the demon bashing, "Doomed"

Xander: "We've got a rogue Slayer on our hands. Real psycho-killer, too."

Spike: "Sounds serious."

Giles: "It is. What do you know?"

Spike: "What do you need?"

Xander: "Her. Dark hair, this tall, name of Faith, criminally insane . . ."

Giles: "Have you seen her?"

Spike: "This bird after you?"

Xander: "In a bad way, yeah."

Spike: "Tell you what I'll do, then. Head out, find this girl, tell her exactly where all of you are, and then watch as she kills you. Can't anyone in your damned little Scooby Club remember that I HATE YOU ALL?!? And just because I can't do the damage myself doesn't stop me from aiming a loose cannon your way."

Xander: "Go ahead—you wouldn't even recognize her anyway."

Spike: "Dark hair, this tall, name of Faith, criminally insane—I like this girl already."

Xander: (to Giles) "We're dumb."

—"This Year's Girl"

"Have you heard, they call him 'William the Bloody' because of his bloody awful poetry."

—Partygoer, "Fool for Love"

"I've seen you. A man surrounded by fools who cannot see his strength. His vision. His glory. That, and burning baby fish swimming all round your head."

—Drusilla, "Fool for Love"

"Come on. *I'm* badder than you."

**—Dawn, who can't be fooled by Spike,
"Blood Ties"**

Buffy: "You have a crush on Spike."
Dawn: "No, I don't! It's just he's got cool hair and he wears cool leather coats and stuff."

—"Crush"

Anya: "Xander, I think you may have hurt [Spike's] feelings."
Xander: "And you should never hurt the feelings of a brutal killer. . . . Actually, that's pretty good advice."

—"Crush"

Spike: "I've changed, Buffy."
Buffy: "You mean the chip? That's not change. That's just holding you back. You're like a serial killer in prison."
Spike: "Women marry them all the time."

—"Crush"

Spike: "[Buffy's] upset about her mum, and if she turns to me for comfort . . . well, I'm not gonna deny it to her. I'm not a monster."

Xander: "Yes! You are a monster. Vampires are monsters! They make monster movies about them!"

Spike: "Well, yeah. Got me there."

—"Intervention"

Buffy: "Listen, skirt-girl. We're not going to 'save' [Spike]. We're going to 'kill' him. He knows who the Key is and there's no way he's not telling Glory."

Buffybot: "You're right. He's evil. Killing him is the only way. We're the Slayer and that's what we do. . . . But you should see him naked. I mean, really. Can we save him now, please?"

—"Intervention"

"I do remember what I said. The promise. To protect [Dawn]. If I'd done that . . . even if I didn't make it, you wouldn't've had to jump." (beat) "I want you to know I did save you. Not when it counted, a' course. But after that. Every night after that. I'd see it all again, do something different. Faster or more clever, you know? Dozens of times, lots of different ways . . . Every night I save you."

—Spike re: Buffy's resurrection, "After Life"

"When I want your opinion, Spike, I . . . will never want your opinion."

> **—Giles, "Once More, with Feeling"**

Buffy: "I kill your kind."

Spike: "And I bite yours. So why don't I want to bite you? And why am I fighting other vampires? I must be a noble vampire. A good guy. On a mission of redemption. I help the hopeless. I'm a vampire with a soul!"

Buffy: "Oh, my God, 'a vampire with a soul'? How lame is that?"

> **—Spike doesn't realize he ain't the original, "Tabula Rasa"**

Spike: "Do you trust me?"

Buffy: "Never."

> **—"Dead Things"**

Buffy: "We missed the bed again."

Spike: "Lucky for the bed."

Buffy: "Is this a new rug?"

Spike: "No. It just looks different when you're under it."

Buffy: "This place is okay for a hole in the ground. You fixed it up."

Spike: "I ate a decorator once. Maybe something stuck."

> **—"Dead Things"**

"You don't have a soul! There's nothing good or clean in you. That's why you can't understand! You're dead inside! You can't feel anything real! I could never . . . be your girl."

—Buffy, "Dead Things"

"It's no wonder they couldn't deal with the likes of you and me, luv. We both should have been dead hundreds of years ago—and we're the only ones that are really alive."

—Spike commiserating with Anya, "Entropy"

Buffy: "It just happened, okay?"
Xander: "Oh, like, 'Say, you're evil. Get on me'?"
Buffy: "Xander, you fought side by side with him when I was gone. You let him take care of Dawn."
Xander: "But I never forgot what he really is."

—"Seeing Red"

"I was the enemy, then I was nothing, and now I'm God's garbage, not even a joke, less than, less than, less than all His creatures combined, so tell me, dear Buffy, how ya like me now?"

—Spike, "Beneath You"

Anya: "You know, you're more fun without the soul."

Spike: "Oh, come on now. I just explained to you—"

Anya: "I'm only saying, Soulless Spike woulda had me upside down and halfway to Happy Land by now."

—**"Sleeper"**

"This chip is something they did to me. I couldn't help it. But the soul I got on my own. For you."
—**Spike to Buffy, "Sleeper"**

Anya: "[Spike's] not done being dangerous. Buffy, you keep him around, you're taking on a huge project."

Xander: "But it'll be fun. No, wait. I mean it'll get us killed."

—**"Sleeper"**

"Soul's not all about moonbeams and penny whistles, love. . . . It's about self-loathing. I get it. Had to travel around the world, but I understand now. I understand the violence inside."
—**Spike to Buffy, "Never Leave Me"**

"Do you know how much blood you can drink from a girl before she'll die? I do. . . . See, the trick is, if you drink just enough . . . know how to damage them *just enough* so that they'll still cry when you . . . Because it isn't worth it if they can't cry."

—Spike to Buffy, "Never Leave Me"

"You faced the monster in you, and you fought back. You risked everything so you could be a better man. And you can be. You are. You may not see it, but I do."

—Buffy to Spike, "Never Leave Me"

Faith: "He's like Angel?"

Spike: "No."

Buffy: "Sort of."

Spike: "I'm nothing like Angel."

Buffy: "He fights on my side. Which is more than I can say for some of us."

Spike: (it's bugging him) "Angel's dull as a table lamp. And we have very different coloring."

—"Dirty Girls"

☉Z

Devon: "What does a girl have to do to impress you?"

Oz: "Well, it involves a feather boa and the theme from *A Summer Place*. I can't discuss it here."

—**"Inca Mummy Girl"**

Willow: "Well, don't you have some ambition?"

Oz: "Oh, yeah. E flat, diminished ninth. The E flat's doable, but it's that diminished ninth . . . that's a *man's* chord. You could lose a finger."

—**"What's My Line? Part Two"**

"I'm gonna ask you if you wanna go out tomorrow night. I'm actually kind of nervous about it. It's interesting."

—**Oz to Willow, "Surprise"**

Oz: "Did everybody else see a guy turn into dust?"

Willow: "Uh, well, uh . . . sort of."

Xander: "Yep. Vampires are real. A lot of them live in Sunnydale. Willow will fill you in."

Willow: "I know it's hard to accept at first."

Oz: "Actually, it explains a lot."

—**Taking it rather well, "Surprise"**

Willow: "You came to visit me!" (puzzled) "You came with books. Are they books for me?"

Oz: "Actually, they're kind of for me."

Willow: "I don't get it."

Oz: "Well, it's sort of a funny story. Remember when I didn't graduate?"

Willow: "Well, I know you had a lot of incompletes, but that's why you had summer school."

Oz: "Yeah. Remember when I didn't go?"

—**"Anne"**

Buffy: "We have a jazz marching band?"

Oz: "Yeah. But—you know—good jazz is improvisational. So we'd be marching off in all different directions. Running into floats and stuff. Scary."

Willow: "He's just being Oz."

Oz: "Pretty much full time."

—**"Beauty and the Beasts"**

Giles: "Clearly we're looking for a depraved, sadistic animal."

Oz: "Present." (glances at Willow) "Hey. I may be a cold-blooded jelly donut—but my timing's impeccable."

—**"Beauty and the Beasts"**

"As Willow goes, so goes my nation."

—**Oz, "Homecoming"**

"You've got great hair."
> **—Principal Snyder to Oz, "Band Candy"**

Xander: "What is the essence of cool?"
Oz: "Not sure."
Xander: "I mean, you yourself, Oz, are considered more or less cool. Why is that?"
Oz: "Am I?"
Xander: "Is it about the talking? You know, the way you tend to express yourself in short, noncommittal phrases?"
Oz: "Could be."
> **—"The Zeppo"**

Xander: "Is it hard to play guitar?"
Oz: "Not the way I play it."
> **—"The Zeppo"**

Devon: "We gotta get a roadie. Other bands have roadies."
Oz: "Other bands know more than three chords. Your professional bands can play up to six and sometimes seven completely different chords."
Devon: "That's just like, fruity jazzy bands."
> **—"Doppelgangland"**

Willow: "Promise me you'll never be linear."
Oz: "On my trout."
> **—"Choices"**

Willow: "If we need to make ferns invisible or communicate with shrimp, I've got the goods right here."

Oz: "Our lives are different than other people's."
—"Graduation Day, Part One"

Cordelia: "Okay, well, I personally don't think it's possible to come up with a **crazier** plan."

Oz: "We attack the Mayor with hummus."

Cordelia: "I stand corrected."

Oz: "Just keeping things in perspective."
—On stopping the Ascension, "Graduation Day, Part Two"

Buffy: "I cannot believe this. After all we've been through together, you won't listen when I tell you that Kathy is bad!"

Xander: "We want to, Buff. It's just—"

Oz: "Don't engage. I'm pretty sure the next part is about fava beans and a nice Chianti."
—"The Freshman"

"Nobody deserves mime, Buffy."
—Not even the irritating Kathy-roommate; Oz, "The Freshman"

Oz: "Okay, I'm either borrowing all your albums or I'm moving in."

Giles: "Oz, there are more important things than records right now."

Oz: "More important than this one?"

Giles: "Yes, well, I suppose an argument could be made . . ."

—**"The Harsh Light of Day"**

"I know what it's like to have power you can't control. Every time I start to wolf out, I touch something deep, dark. . . . It's not fun."

—**Oz, "Fear, Itself"**

Oz: "You got a table."

Willow: "I had to kill a man."

Oz: "Well, it's a really good table."

—**"Beer Bad"**

Oz: "Veruca was right about something. The wolf is inside me all the time. And I don't know where the line is anymore—between me and it. Until I figure out what that means, I shouldn't be around you—or anybody."

Willow: "That could be a problem. 'Cause people? Pretty much a planetary epidemic."

—**"Wild at Heart"**

"Oz? Are you all right? If possible, you seem even more monosyllabic than usual."

—Buffy, "Wild at Heart"

Veruca: "You have a cage?"
Oz: "Don't you?"
Veruca: "Yeah. It has a little wheel and a cute plastic ball with a bell in it."

—"Wild at Heart"

"I went through a lot of changes while we were apart. I know what I put you through. And I'm not going to push . . . But I'm a different person than when I left. I can be what you need now. And that's what I want."

—Oz to Willow, "New Moon Rising"

Willow: "It's light out. What time is it?"
Oz: "Almost eight. We talked all night."
Willow: "I used to tell people we did that sometimes, but nobody believed you knew that many words."

—"New Moon Rising"

Willow: "I missed you, Oz. I wrote you so many letters—but I didn't have any place to send them, you know? I couldn't live like that."

Oz: "It was stupid to think you'd just be waiting."

Willow: "I *was* waiting. I feel like some part of me will always be waiting for you. Like, if I'm old and blue-haired and I turn a corner in Istanbul and there you are—I won't be surprised. Because you're with me—you know?"

—"New Moon Rising"

ΛΠΥΛ

"For a thousand years I wielded the power of the wish. I brought ruin upon the heads of unfaithful men, I offered destruction and chaos for the pleasure of lower beings. I was feared and worshipped across the mortal globe and now I'm stuck at Sunnydale High! A mortal! A child! And I'm flunking math!"

—Mortality bites; Anya, "Doppelgangland"

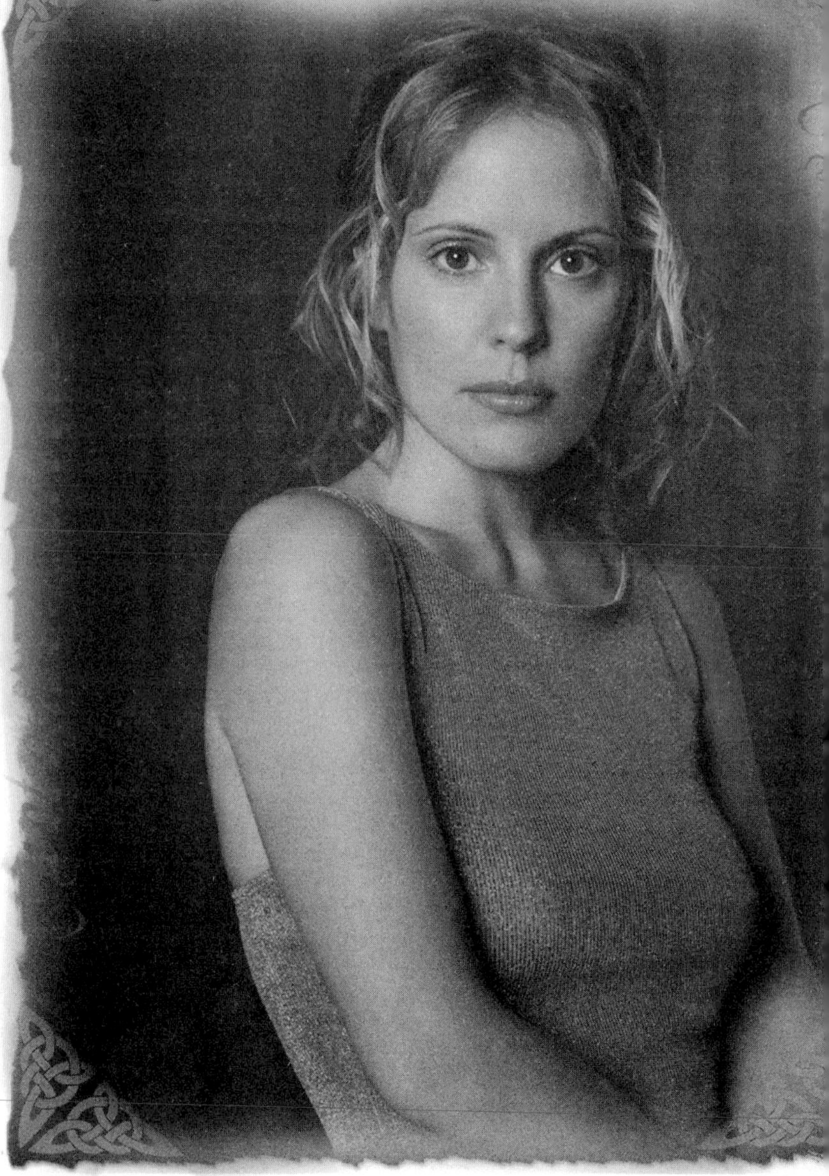

Anya: "Gimme a beer."

Waiter: "ID."

Anya: "I'm eleven hundred and twenty years old! Just give me a friggin' beer!"

Waiter: "ID."

Anya: "Give me a Coke."

—**A rough day, "Doppelgangland"**

Anya: "You can laugh, but I have witnessed a millennium of treachery and oppression from the males of the species. I have nothing but contempt for the whole libidinous lot of them."

Xander: "Then why are you talking to me?"

Anya: "I don't have a date for the prom."

Xander: "And, gosh, I wonder why not. Can't possibly have anything to do with your sales pitch. . . ."

Anya: "Men are evil. . . . Will you go with me?"

Xander: "One of us is very confused, and I honestly don't know which."

—**"Choices"**

Xander: "You'll need a costume."

Anya: "A costume?"

Xander: "Dress up. You know, something scary."

Anya: "Scary. Scary how?"

Xander: "Anya, you—ex-demon—terrorized mankind for centuries. I'm sure you'll come up with something."

—**"Fear, Itself"**

Anya: "Are you listening? Xander's trapped!"

Giles: "Where are Buffy and the others?"

Anya: "Oh. They're trapped too. . . . But we have to save Xander!"

—**"Fear, Itself"**

Willow: "I think he thought we were crazy."

Xander: "Maybe Anya shouldn't have opened the conversation with, 'Everybody got both ears?'"

—**Subtlety, thy name is Anya, "Pangs"**

"I like my money the way it is when it's mine."

—**Anya, "Where the Wild Things Are"**

"A year and a half ago I could have eviscerated [Xander] with my thoughts. Now I can barely hurt his feelings. Things used to be so much simpler."

—**Anya, "Where the Wild Things Are"**

"I've been thinking about getting back into vengeance. You know, I miss it, I'm so at loose ends since I quit, and I think this is gonna be a very big year for vengeance. I've been keeping close tabs on cultural trends—a lot of men being unfaithful—very exciting things happening in the scorned-women market. I don't wanna be left out."

—Anya, "Restless"

Anya: "Oh, crap. Look at this. Now I am burdened with a husband and several tiny pink children and more cash than I can reasonably manage."

Xander: "That means you're winning."

Anya: "Really?"

Xander: "Yes. Cash equals good."

Anya: "Oh, I'm so pleased! Can I trade in the children for more cash?"

—Mastering the game of Life, "Real Me"

Anya: "I'm nearly out of money. I've never had to 'afford' things before, and it's making me bitter."

Giles: "And the change is palpable."

—"No Place Like Home"

"I, for one, wasn't looking forward to starting my day with a slaughter." (thoughtfully, pleased with herself) "Which, really, just goes to show how much I've grown."

—**Anya, "Shadow"**

"Oh, yes. Very humorous. Make fun of the ex-demon. I can just hear you in private: 'I dislike that Anya. She is newly human and strangely literal.'"

—**Anya, "Into the Woods"**

"Have a nice day. Don't get killed!"

—**Anya, "Into the Woods"**

"I need to say something to you I should have said a long time ago. I mean, you may not even know . . . I love you, Anya, more every day. I love the way you see things. I love the way you work a cash register and how beautiful you are, and how amazingly sweet and crazy you can be at the same time. . . . I can't imagine my days without you—and I wouldn't want to."

—**Xander, "Into the Woods"**

"I like money better than people. People can so rarely be exchanged for goods and/or services."

—**Willow imitating Anya, "Triangle"**

"Anya Christina Emmanualla Jenkins. Twenty years old. Born on the fourth of July, and don't think there weren't jokes about that my whole life, mister, 'cause there were. 'Who's our little patriot?' they'd say when I was younger and therefore smaller and shorter than I am now. And when I was seven, I had a pet dachshund that died from choking on a wiener, which I find ironic."

> **—Anya, checking in with the Watchers Council, "Checkpoint"**

Lydia: "We're talking about children."
Buffy: "I'm talking about two powerful witches and a thousand-year-old ex-demon."
Anya: "Willow's a DEMON?"

> **—Still with the covering, "Checkpoint"**

Tara: "Willow's good at all that computer stuff, but me, not so much. You really understand it all?"
Anya: "Oh, at first it was confusing. Just the idea of computers was like—whoa, I'm eleven hundred years old here; I had trouble adjusting to the idea of Lutherans."

> **—"I Was Made to Love You"**

Anya: "Tara and I met [April]. She speaks with a strange evenness and selects her words a shade too precisely."

Xander: "Some of us like that kind of thing in a girl."

—"I Was Made to Love You"

Anya: "Do you think we should set up lots of candles at Buffy's party tomorrow?"

Xander: "Not if they're that horrible slug kind you keep trying to unload."

Anya: "I don't know why people get so turned off by slug."

Xander: "Honey, slugs get turned off by slug."

—"Older and Far Away"

"I, Anya, promise to love you, to cherish you, and to honor you, but not to obey you, of course, because that's anachronistic and misogynistic and who do you think you are, like a sea captain or something? I will, however, entrust you with my heart. Take care of my heart, won't you please? Take care of it, because it's all that I have. And if you let me, I'll take care of your heart too. I'll protect it and tend to it like a little mangy stray that needs a home."

—Anya's vows, take one, "Hell's Bells"

Anya: "I promise to cherish you . . . Eew, no! 'Cherish'? I promise to have sex with you whenever . . . *I* want, and pledge to be your friend and your wife and your confidant and your sex poodle and—"

Tara: "Sex poodle?"

Anya: "Yeah, why?"

Tara: "Um, I'm not sure you should say 'sex poodle' in your vows."

Anya: "Huh."

—Take two, "Hell's Bells"

Anya: "I want to see Xander now!"

Willow: "You can't. It's bad luck for the groom to see the bride in her dress, 'member?"

Anya: "Oh, I can't keep all these ridiculous traditions straight. . . . What if I'm not wearing my dress when I see him . . . ? Okay, no sex."

—"Hell's Bells"

Spike: "I was always going above and beyond. I saved the Scoobies how many times? And I can't stand the lot of you."

Anya: "Me either! I hate us!"

—"Entropy"

Anya: "I wish your intestines were twisted into knots and ripped apart inside your lousy gut!"

Xander: "They are."

Anya: "Really? Right now . . . ? Does it hurt?"

Xander: "God, yes. It hurts so bad it's killing me. Anya, I love you. I want to make this work."

Anya: "Those are metaphor intestines! You're not in real pain!"

—**"Entropy"**

Anya: "[Willow] tried to use you as a hood ornament, Xander. She doesn't care if you live or die."

Xander: "Guess you two finally have something in common."

Anya: "I care if you live or die, Xander. I'm just not sure which one I want."

—**"Two to Go"**

Hallie: "Waitress downtown wished her husband was a frog, you made him French!"

Anya: "Well that's a . . . he's smelly, and with the little moustache . . ."

—**On going soft, "Lessons"**

"Here's a little something you should know about Vengeance Demons. We don't groove with the 'sorry.' We prefer the 'Oh, God, please stop hitting me with my own rib bones!'"

—**Anya, "Same Time, Same Place"**

Anya: "I'm surprisingly sensitive."

Willow: "So . . . will you help me?"

Anya: "Is it difficult or time-consuming?"

—**"Same Time, Same Place"**

"I don't talk to people much. I mean, I talk to them, but they don't talk to me. Except to say, 'Your questions are irksome' and 'Perhaps you should take your furs and your literal interpretations to the other side of the river.'"

—**Pre-demon days aren't so different from post; Anya, "Selfless"**

Anya: "What if I'm really nobody?"

Xander: "Don't be a dope."

Anya: "I'm a dope?"

Xander: "Sometimes."

Anya: "Well, that's a start."

—**"Selfless"**

Anya: "Well, if Spike is biting people then there should be more dead people with neck trauma, right? We can find that."

Willow: "No."

Anya: "We can't find that? But that's easy. That computer is a moron."

—**"Sleeper"**

"I was kinda new to being around humans before. And now I've seen a lot more, gotten to know people, seen what they're capable of, and I realize now that they're just so . . . amazingly . . . screwed up! I mean, so really, really screwed up in a monumental fashion! They have no purpose that unites them, so they drift around, blundering through life until they die. Which they *know* is coming, and yet every single one of them is surprised when it happens to them. They're incapable of thinking beyond what they want at that moment. They kill *each other,* which is *clearly* insane, but here's the thing. When it's something real, they fight. I mean, they're lame morons to keep fighting. But they do. They . . . They never quit. And so I guess I'll fight too."

—Anya, "End of Days"

Andrew: "She was incredible. She died saving my life."
Xander: (welling up) "That's my girl. Always doing the stupid thing."

—Anya's fate, "End of Days"

RİLEY

"Don't make fun. I worked long and hard to get this pompous."

—Riley, "Fear, Itself"

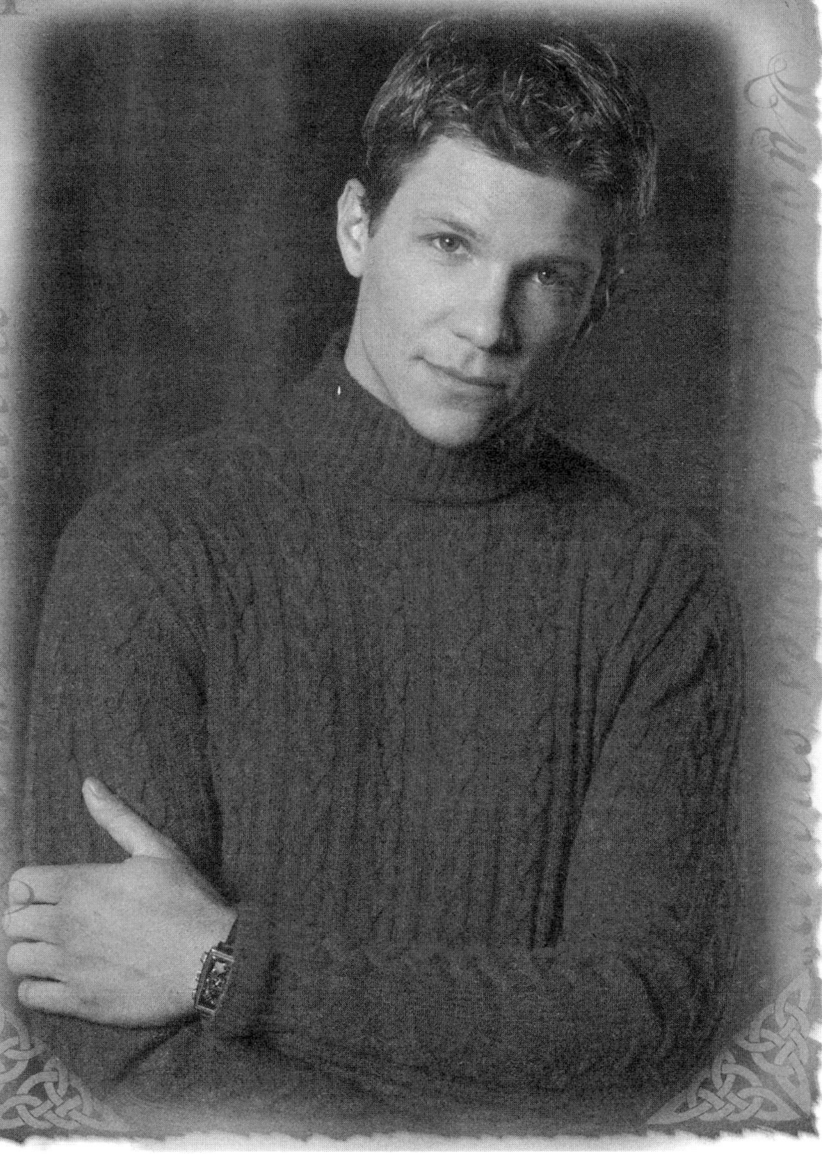

Riley: "After dinner, we all go for a walk down by the river with the dogs. And there's . . . trees, and I know what you're thinking: It's like I grew up in a Grant Wood painting."

Buffy: "Exactly. If I knew who that was."

—The life of Riley, "Pangs"

Colonel McNamara: "You're a dead man, Finn."

Riley: "No sir—I'm an anarchist."

—"New Moon Rising"

Riley: "I'm sorry to just drop in on you like this, Buffy."

Buffy: "It's you."

Riley: "It's me."

Buffy: "You're here."

Riley: "I know."

Buffy: "And . . . were you always this tall?"

—A reunion, "As You Were"

Quotable Scoobies

Willow: "Buffy's like my best friend, and she's really special, plus, you know, Slayer, and that's a deal, and there's a whole bunch of us, and we have this group thing that kind of revolves around the slaying and I really want you to meet them and meet Buffy but I just sort of like having something that's just, you know, mine. I don't usually use that many words to say stuff that little. But do you get it at all?"

Tara: "I do. I am, you know."

Willow: "What?"

Tara: "Yours."

—"Who Are You"

Willow: "Tara, I have to tell you that—"

Tara: "I understand. You have to be with the person you love."

Willow: "I am."

Tara: "You mean—"

Willow: "I mean. Okay?"

Tara: "Oh, yes."

—"New Moon Rising"

Buffy: "You don't know how hard it is. Lying to everyone you love about who you're sleeping with."

Tara: "Sweetie, I'm a fag. I been there."

—"Dead Things"

95

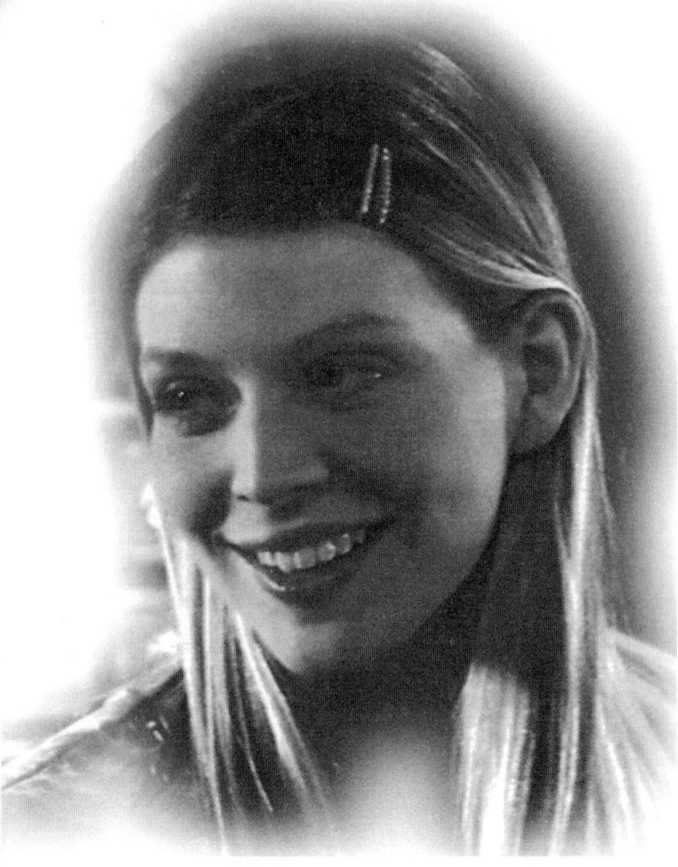

Tara: "You know it takes time. You can't just have coffee and expect—"

Willow: "I know."

Tara: "There's so much to work through. Trust has to build again, on both sides. . . . You have to learn if you're even the same people you were, if you can fit in each other's lives. It's a long and important process and can we just skip it? Can you just be kissing me now?"

—Reconciliation, "Entropy"

DAWN

"I could *so* save the world if somebody handed *me* superpowers. But I'd think of a cool name and wear a mask to protect my loved ones, which Buffy doesn't even."

—Dawn, "Real Me"

"I can't help it. I have all this involuntary empathy for Dawn, 'cause she's, you know, a big spazz."

—Willow, "No Place Like Home"

Dawn: "Like you'd tell me [anything] anyway. 'Dawn's too young.' ' Dawn's too delicate.' "

Buffy: "Right. A young delicate pain in the butt."

—"Blood Ties"

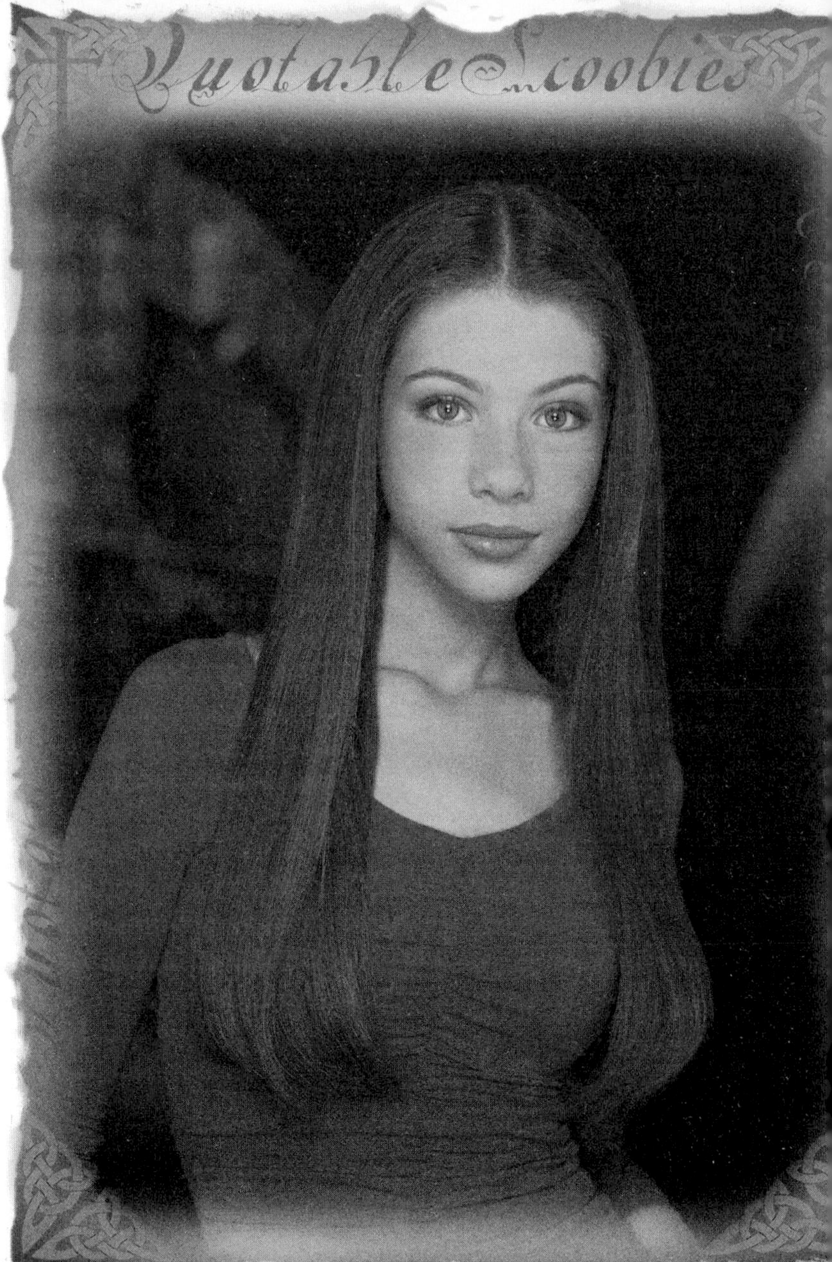
Quotable Scoobies

Xander: "You know, [Dawn]'s, uh, she's kinda got a crush on me."

Giles: "Your point being?"

Xander: "Well, no, nothing. I'm just saying, powerful being, big important energy gal, diggin' the Xan-man. Some guys are just cooler, ya know."

—"Blood Ties"

"It doesn't matter how you got here or where you came from. You are my sister. There's no way you could annoy me as much if you weren't."

—Buffy, "Blood Ties"

Buffy: "What did she make you do?"

Giles: "Well, we listened to some aggressively cheerful music sung by people chosen for their ability to dance, then we ate cookie dough and talked about boys."

—Adventures in baby-sitting, "I Was Made to Love You"

Buffy: "All right. Nobody goes home, nobody tells anyone we're leaving. We grab whatever supplies we can and that's it—gone."

Dawn: "Cool. Won't have to study for that geometry test."

—"Spiral"

Xander: "[Dawn]'s all confusing. Stay here. Go away."

Anya: "I think she's possessed."

Buffy: "That'd be nice."

        —Teen angst, "Older and Far Away"

Dawn: "I was there, remember? I hear you when I'm in the room, you know. I do understand these things."

Anya: "Yes, you do."

Dawn: "You know I'm in high school, right?"

Anya: "Yes, you are."

        —"Older and Far Away"

"People keep—people have a tendency to go away. And I miss them. And sometimes I wish I could make them stop. Going away."

        —Dawn, "Older and Far Away"

Dawn: "Why don't I come patrolling with you tonight?"

Buffy: "Uh huh. And then maybe we'll invite over some strangers and ask them to feed you candy."

        —"Entropy"

Buffy: "Hey, you didn't steal anything from the pet store, did you?"

Dawn: "Pocketful of goldfish. Didn't work out."

        —"Entropy"

Buffy: "You stole a toothbrush?"

Dawn: "Mother of pearl handle. Very fancy."

Buffy: "Yeah, but you stole a *toothbrush*. As rebellious teenagers go, you're kinda square."

Dawn: "Dental hygiene is important."

—**"Entropy"**

"Things have sucked lately, but it's all gonna change—and I want to see my friends happy again. And I want to see you grow up. The woman you're going to become . . . because she's going to be beautiful. And she's going to be powerful. I got it so wrong. I don't want to protect you from the world—I want to show it to you."

—**Buffy to Dawn, "Grave"**

Buffy: "Let me see."

Dawn: "Just a scrape. Anyway, I had a plan the whole time."

Buffy: "Really."

Dawn: "Yeah, I planned to get killed, come back as a vampire, and bite you."

—**"Lessons"**

"My sister is a vampire slayer, her best friend is a witch who went bonkers and tried to destroy the world. Um, I actually used to be a little ball of energy until about two years ago when some monks changed the past and made me Buffy's sister, and for some reason, a big klepto. My best friends are Leticia Jones, who moved to San Diego because this town is evil, and a floppy-eared demon named Clem."

—Introductions, the daydream version; Dawn, "Lessons"

"I love to dance. I love music. I'm very into Britney Spears's early work, you know, before she sold out, so mostly her finger painting, macaroni art. Very underrated. Favorite activities include not ever having to do this again."

—Introductions, the real version; Dawn, "Lessons"

"It's just so cool. You're coming to school with me! You'll be, like, right there, the whole time. . . . You understand you can never talk to me, look at me, or hang out anywhere near my friends, right?"

—Dawn to Buffy, "Beneath You"

Dawn: "You sleep, right? You. Vampires. You sleep."

Spike: "Yeah. What's your point, niblet?"

Dawn: "Well, I couldn't take you in a fight or anything, even with that chip in your head. But you do sleep. And if you hurt my sister, *at all,* if you *touch* her—you're gonna wake up on fire."

—**"Beneath You"**

Buffy: "[Willow] was about to kill Dawn!"

Dawn: "I didn't care for it."

—**"Same Time, Same Place"**

"Will anyone around here ever ask for help when they need it? Instead everyone just keeps secrets, and suffers alone, and then we're s'posed to be all sympathetic when they start ripping the skins off people or dragging their sisters into the basement! . . . I may have some stuff to work through."

—**Dawn, "Same Time, Same Place"**

Dawn: "Anything else gone? Eyeballs or toenails or viscera? That's guts."

Buffy: "She knows about viscera. Makes you proud."

—**"Same Time, Same Place"**

Buffy: "It's pretty easy. Spike follows the exciting smell of blood. We follow the fairly ripe smell of Spike."

Dawn: "It's smellementary!"

          —"Same Time, Same Place"

Dawn: "I bet there's tons of stuff like this, procedures we can use that don't involve magic spells, just good solid detective work. Like, we could develop a database of tooth impressions and demon-skin samples. And I could wear high heels more."

Buffy: "Wow, that was so close to being empowering."

Dawn: "Well, everyone wants a slender ankle."

          —"Same Time, Same Place"

"People may say something you don't understand. Don't be afraid to keep your mouth shut and pretend like you know what they're talking about. They may say something like 'My protein window closes in an hour.' Just smile and nod."

          —Dawn, re: high school, "Selfless"

R. J.: "I heard Wood hauled you into his office."
Dawn: "Well, yeah."
R. J.: "That sucks. Facing the whole inquisition thing."
Dawn: "Yeah, no one expects the Spanish Inquisition. . . ."

—"Him"

"Oh my god. I'm the Pushy Queen of Sluttown."
—Dawn, after making the first move, "Him"

"I saw what you did last night. Thought you were all special. Miss Sunnydale, 2003. And the minute you found out you weren't, you handed the crown over without a moment's pause. You gave [away] your power. They'll never know how tough it is, Dawnie. To be the one who **isn't** chosen; to live so near the spotlight and never step in it. But I know. I see more than anybody realizes, 'cause nobody's watching me. I saw you last night, I saw you working here today. . . . You're not special. You're extraordinary."

—Xander to Dawn, "Potential"

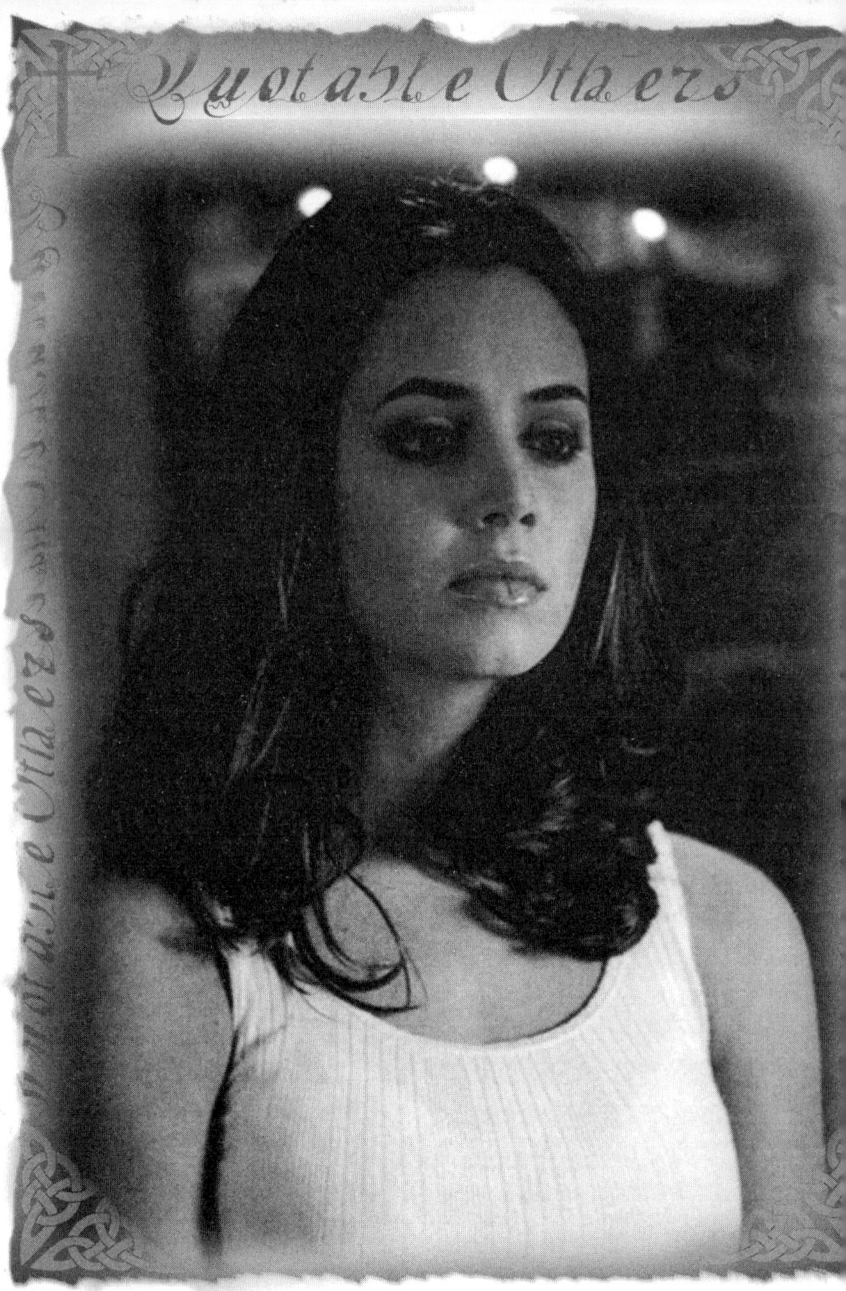

QUOTABLE
OTHER PEOPLE

FAITH

Faith: "—It was about a hundred and eighteen
degrees, I'm sleepin' without a stitch on,
suddenly I hear all this screamin'. I go
tearin' outside—stark nude—this church
bus has broke down and three vamps are
feasting on half the Baptists in South
Boston. So I waste the vamps and the
preacher is hugging me like there's no
tomorrow when the cops pull up. They
arrested us both."

Xander: "They should film that story and show it
every Christmas."

**—The start of a beautiful
relationship, "Faith, Hope & Trick"**

"You guys are a hoot and a half. If I'd had friends like you in high school, I'd've still dropped out, but I mighta been sad about it."

> —Faith to Xander and Willow,
> "Faith, Hope & Trick"

"Faith, a word of advice. You're an idiot."

> —Gwendolyn Post, "Revelations"

Angel: "You're not alive. You're just running. Afraid to feel. Afraid to be touched . . ."

Faith: "Save it for Hallmark. I have to pee."

> —"Consequences"

Wesley: "Wait for Faith."

Buffy: "That could be hours. The girl makes Godot look punctual."

> —"Enemies"

"It didn't have to be this way, but you made your choice. I know you've had a tough life. I know some people think you've had a lot of bad breaks and that you've hardened your heart to protect yourself from the pain. . . . Well, boo-hoo. Poor you. You had a lot more in your life than some people. You had friends like Buffy. Now you've got no one. And you were a slayer! One of the Chosen. Now you're nothing. Just a selfish, worthless waste."

> —Willow, "Choices"

"You look lovely. Perfect for the Ascension. Any boys that manage to survive'll be lining up to ask you out."

> **—The Mayor, re: Faith in a Dress!,**
> **"Graduation Day, Part One"**

Giles: "Faith has you at a disadvantage, Buffy."
Buffy: "'Cause I'm not crazy or 'cause I don't kill people?"
Giles: "Both, actually."

> **—"Graduation Day, Part One"**

"Why, yes, I would be Buffy. May I help you?"
> **—Faith in Buffy's skin, "Who Are You"**

"You can't do that. That would be wrong. Hey. I'm Buffy Summers, I'll kick your ass with my righteous fiery Slayerness. You can't do that. Because it's naughty. Because it's wrong."

> **—Faith, imitating Buffy, "Who Are You"**

Spike:	"You know why I really hate you, Summers?"
Faith:	"I'm a stuck-up tight-ass with no sense of fun?"
Spike:	"Wuh—yeah, that . . . covers a lot of it. . . ."
Faith:	"'Cause I could do anything I want and instead I just pout and whine and feel the burden of Slayerness? I mean, I could be rich, I could be famous, I could have anything. Anyone. Even you, Spike. I could ride you at a gallop till your legs buckled and your eyes rolled up. I've got muscles you've never even dreamed up; I could squeeze you till you popped like warm champagne and you'd beg me to hurt you just a little bit more. And you know why I don't? Because it's wrong."

> **—Faith, as Buffy, "Who Are You"**

"Guess you really never know a person till you've been inside their skin."

> **—Faith on lessons learned as Buffy, "Who Are You"**

"Oh, you wouldn't have liked Faith. She's not proper and joyless like a girl should be. She has a tendency to give in to her animal instincts."

> **—A third-person perspective from a Slayer in Buffy's clothing; Faith, "Who Are You"**

"You protecting vampires? Are you the bad Slayer now? Am I the good Slayer now?"

—**Faith to Buffy, "Dirty Girls"**

WESLEY

Buffy: "New Watcher?"
Giles: "New Watcher."
Buffy: "Is he evil?"
Giles: "Not in the strictest sense."

—**"Bad Girls"**

Faith: "New Watcher?"
Buffy and Giles: "New Watcher."
Faith: "Screw that."

—**"Bad Girls"**

"Check out Giles, the next generation."
—**Cordelia, on spotting Wesley, "Consequences"**

"Well then, yes. In fact I am. Here to watch. Girls. I mean Buffy and Faith, in specific."

—**Wesley, "Consequences"**

Wesley: "I must say, it's all rather odd to me."

Giles: "Yes. Being at an all-male preparatory, we didn't go in for this sort of thing."

Wesley: "No. Of course not. Unless you count the nights you made the lower-classmen get up as girls and—Dip is tasty, isn't it?"

—On the prom, "Choices"

Cordelia: "I demand an explanation."

Xander: "For what?"

Cordelia: "Wesley!"

Xander: "Um . . . inbreeding?"

—"Graduation Day, Part Two"

Giles: "Buffy no longer needs a Watcher."

Cordelia: "Well, does he have to leave the country? I mean, you got fired and you hang around like a big loser, why can't he?"

—"Graduation Day, Part Two"

OTHER OTHERS

Ford: "I wanna be like you. A vampire."

Spike: "I've known you for two minutes and I can't stand you. I don't really feature you living forever."

—"Lie to Me"

Kendra: "I'm the Slayer."

Buffy: "Nice cover story. Here's a tip—try it on someone who's not the real Slayer."

—"What's My Line? Part Two"

"This is our year, I'm telling you. Best football season ever. I'm so in shape, I'm a rock—it's all about egg whites—we got Garrity at running back, Dale at QB, if we can focus, keep discipline, and not have quite as many mysterious deaths, Sunnydale is gonna RULE."

—Larry, "Anne"

"It's just . . . You never really know what's going on inside somebody—do you? You think if you care about them—you know. But you never really do."

—Scott Hope, "Beauty and the Beasts"

"Call me Snyder. Just a last name. Like Barbarino. Whoo! I'm stoked! Did you see Ms. Barton? I think she's wasted. I'm gonna put that on her next performance review because I'm the principal."

—Principal Snyder, "Band Candy"

Bob: "How long I been down?"

Jack: "Eight months, bro. Had to wait for the stars to align."

Bob: "Eight months! Man. I got some catching up to do. . . . You been taping *Walker, Texas Ranger*?"

— **On being dead, "The Zeppo"**

Snyder: "Okay, what's in the bag?"

Student: "My lunch."

Snyder: "Oh, is that the new drug lingo?"

Student: "It's my lunch."

Snyder: "Sit up straight."

—**"Choices"**

"I wear the cheese. It does not wear me."

—**The Cheese Man, "Restless"**

"That'll put marzipan in your pie plate, Bingo!"

—**The Buffybot, "Bargaining, Part One"**

Xander: "You met Krelvin already, Dad. Last night."

Warty Demon: "Yes. We met. You said I resembled your mother-in-law."

Mr. Harris: "Oh, yeah."

Warty Demon: "Later you hit me with a cocktail wiener and insulted my heritage."

—**"Hell's Bells"**

...Buffy on...

BUFFY ON . . .

SLAYING

"It's my first day. I was afraid that I'd be behind on all my classes, that I wouldn't make any friends, that I'd have last month's hair. I didn't think there would be vampires on campus."

—Buffy, "Welcome to the Hellmouth"

Giles: "Into every generation, a Slayer is born. One girl in all the world, a Chosen One. One born with the—

Buffy and Giles: "—the strength and skill to hunt the vampires—"

Buffy: "To stop the spread of their evil blah blah I've **heard** it, okay?"

—"Welcome to the Hellmouth"

Giles: "As long as there have been vampires, there has been the Slayer. One girl in all the world—"

Buffy: "He loves doing this part."

Giles: (speeding up) "All right: They hunt vampires, one Slayer dies, the next is called, Buffy is the Slayer, don't tell anyone. I think that's all the vampire information you need."

—**Breaking it down for Willow and Xander, "The Harvest"**

Xander: "We're a team! Aren't we a team?"

Willow: "Yeah, you're the Slayer and we're like the Slayerettes."

—**"The Witch"**

"I'm not saying your methods are without merit, but you're expending far too much time and energy. It should simply be 'plunge' and move on; 'plunge' and move on."

—**Giles, re: Buffy's technique for making the world safe for humanity again, "Never Kill a Boy on the First Date"**

"A cranky Slayer is a careless Slayer."

—**Buffy, "Never Kill a Boy on the First Date"**

"Giles, *care.* I'm putting my life on the line, battling the undead! I broke a nail, okay? **I'm wearing a press-on.** The least you could do is exhibit some casual interest. . . . You could go, 'Hmmmm.'"

—**Buffy, "Prophecy Girl"**

"You know what I find works real good with Slayers? Killing them."

—**Spike, "School Hard"**

Giles: "When you live atop a mystical convergence it's only a matter of time before a fresh hell breaks loose. Now is the time to train more strictly, hunt and patrol more keenly, hone your skills day and night—"

Buffy: "And the little scrap of my life that still belongs to me—say, from seven to seven-oh-five in the morning—can I do what I want to then?"

Giles: (beat) "Buffy, you think I don't know what it's like to be sixteen?"

Buffy: "I think you don't know what it's like to be sixteen and a girl and a Slayer."

Giles: "Well, I don't."

Buffy: "Or what it's like to stake vampires while you're having fuzzy feelings towards one. Digging on the undead doesn't exactly do wonders for your social life."

—**"Reptile Boy"**

Buffy: "Handbook? What handbook? How come I didn't get a handbook?"

Willow: "Is there a T-shirt, too? 'Cause, that would be cool . . ."

Giles: "After meeting you, Buffy, I was quite sure the handbook would be of no use in your case."

—**"What's My Line? Part Two"**

"Another Slayer? I knew this 'I'm the only one, I'm the only one' thing was just an attention-getter."

—**Xander, re: meeting Kendra, "What's My Line? Part Two"**

Joyce: "A little responsibility, Buffy, that's all I ask. Honestly, don't you ever think about anything besides boys and clothes?"

Buffy: "Saving the world from vampires."

Joyce: "I swear, sometimes I have no idea what goes on in your head."

—**"Bad Eggs"**

Willow: "Well, well, the **Slayer** always says a pun or a witty play on words and I think it throws vampires off and makes them frightened."

Xander: "I was always amazed by the way Buffy fought, but . . . in a way I think we all took her punning for granted."

—**"Anne"**

"We try not to get killed. That's part of our whole mission statement: 'Don't get killed.'"

—Willow, "Anne"

Faith: "When I'm fighting, the whole world goes away and I only know one thing: I'm gonna win, and they're gonna lose. I like that feeling."

Buffy: "Well, sure, it's better than that dead feeling you get when they win and you lose."

—"Faith, Hope & Trick"

Buffy: "Okay. Maybe I don't have a plan. Lord knows I don't have lapel buttons. And maybe the next time the world is getting sucked into hell, I won't be able to stop it because, guess what, the anti-hell-sucking book isn't on the approved reading list!"

Joyce: "I'm sorry. I didn't mean to put down—"

Buffy: "Yeah. You did. But you know what? I have to go. I have to go out on one of my pointless little patrols now, and 'react to' some
vampires, if that's all right with MOO."

—"Gingerbread"

Buffy: "There's a plus side to being a regular girl. The whole not-bleeding-and-killing-and-dying experience."

Willow: "As for example."

Buffy: "Then there's buying outfits without worrying if they're good for bleeding-and-killing-and-dying in. There's a lot of good to it."

—**"Helpless"**

"If I had the Slayer's power . . . I'd be punning right about now."

—**Buffy, "Helpless"**

Wesley: "Remember the three key words for any slayer: Preparation. Preparation. Preparation."

Buffy: "That's one word three times."

—**"Bad Girls"**

Buffy: "You're hurting people. You're hurting yourself."

Faith: "But that's not it. That's not what bothers you so much. What bugs you is you know I'm right. You know in your gut. We don't need the law. We are the law."

—**"Consequences"**

"The way I got it figured, Slayer's like some kind of bogeyman for the Sub-Terrestrials. Something they tell their little spawn to get them to eat their vegetables and clean up their slime pits."

—Forrest, "Doomed"

"You know, when I saw you stop the world from ending, I assumed that was a big week for you. Turns out I suddenly find myself . . . needing to know the plural of apocalypse."

—Riley, "A New Man"

"Same as all the others. Slayer called, blah, blah, blah, scary battles, blah, blah, blah, great protector, blah, blah, bl—oops, she's dead. Where are the details?"

—Buffy, re: less-than-helpful Watcher's Diaries, "Fool for Love"

"I mean, I know every Slayer comes with an expiration mark on the package, but I want mine to be a long time from now. Like a Cheeto . . ."

—Buffy, "Fool for Love"

"We just keep coming. Like a wave of roaches, and here you are doing a minute waltz, trying to stomp us all. But you can kill a hundred. A thousand. A thousand thousand and the armies of Hell besides. But all we need . . . is for one of us, just one, sooner or later, to have the thing we all are hoping for. One. Good. Day."

—Spike, "Fool for Love"

Travers: "The Council fights evil. The Slayer is the instrument with which we fight. The Council remains. The Slayers . . . change. It's been that way from the beginning."

Giles: "Yes, very comforting, bloodless way of looking at it, isn't it?"

—"Checkpoint"

Giles: "I'm not sure our basic workout is challenging you anymore. Perhaps we should make it harder."

Buffy: "You always think harder is better. Maybe next time I patrol, I should carry bricks and use a stake made out of butter."

—"Blood Ties"

Buffy: "So, how does it start?"

Giles: "I jump out of the circle, jump back in, and shake my gourd."

Buffy: "Hey, I think I know this ritual. The ancient shamans were next called upon to do the hokey-pokey and to turn themselves around."

Giles: "Go. Quest."

Buffy: "And that's what it's all about."

—Rituals make great party games, "Intervention"

"What if I stop being able to love people at all? I mean, I slay. Slay equals kill. Maybe being hard is part of the package. Maybe when I finally get to where I'm the perfect Slayer, I will be made of stone."

—Buffy, "Intervention"

"I don't see why we have to patrol just 'cause Buffy's away. I'd rather stay home and watch television. It's often funnier than killing stuff."

—Anya, "Intervention"

Dawn: "Buffy's never gonna be a lawyer. Or a doctor. Anything big."

Xander: "She's the Slayer. She saves the whole world. That's way bigger."

—"Doublemeat Palace"

125

"Isn't that just like a Slayer? Solving all her problems by sticking things with sharp objects."

—**D'Hoffryn, "Selfless"**

"It doesn't have any markings. Would it be so hard to include a little sticker? 'Hello, my name is the Blank of Blankthusela, consult operating instructions before wielding.'"

—**Willow thinks that scythe matters, "End of Days"**

Faith:	"The point? Me, by myself all the time, and looking at you, everything you have, and I don't know . . . jealous. And then there I am, everybody looking to me, trusting me to lead 'em . . . and I never felt more alone in my life. And that's you every day, isn't it?"
Buffy:	"I love my friends, and I'm grateful for them, but yeah, that's the price. Being the Slayer."

—**"End of Days"**

Faith:	"There's only supposed to be one [Slayer]. Maybe that's why you and I can never get along. We're not supposed to exist together."
Buffy:	"Also, you went evil and were killing people."
Faith:	"Good point. Also a factor."

—**"End of Days"**

Buffy: "I guess everyone's alone, but . . . being a Slayer. There's a burden we can't share."

Faith: "And no one else can feel it." (beat) "Thank God we're hot chicks with superpowers."

Buffy: (agreeing) "Takes the edge off."

—**"End of Days"**

AUTHORITY

"Welcome to Sunnydale. A clean slate, Buffy, that's what you get here. What's past is past. We're not interested in what it says on a piece of paper. Even if it says—whoa."
—Principal Flutie reacts to Buffy's permanent record, "Welcome to the Hellmouth"

Joyce: "The tapes all say I should get used to saying it. No."
Buffy: "This is important."
Joyce: "I know. You have to go out or it'll be the end of the world. Everything is life or death when you're a sixteen-year-old girl."
—"The Harvest"

Principal Snyder: "So. We think school events are stupid. And we think authority figures are to be made fun of."
Buffy: "Oh, no! We don't—unless *you* do—"
—"The Puppet Show"

"There are things I will not tolerate. Students loitering on campus after school. Horrible murders with hearts being removed. And also smoking."
—**Principal Snyder, "The Puppet Show"**

"My predecessor, Mr. Flutie, may have gone in for all that touchy-feely relating nonsense. But he was eaten. You're in my world now. Sunnydale has touched and felt for the last time."
—**Principal Snyder, "The Puppet Show"**

Principal Snyder: "It's incredible. One day the campus is completely bare, empty . . . the next, children are everywhere. Like locusts. Crawling around, mindlessly bent on feeding and mating, destroying everything in sight in their relentless, pointless desire to exist."

Giles: "I do love these pep talks. Have you ever considered, given your abhorrence of children, that school principal is perhaps not your true vocation?"
—**"When She Was Bad"**

"Buffy, you acted wrongly, I admit, but believe me, that was hardly the worst mistake you'll ever make." (beat) "That wasn't nearly as comforting as it was meant to be."
—**Giles offers some questionable support, "When She Was Bad"**

"A lot of educators tell students: Think of your principal as your 'pal.' I say, think of me as your judge, jury, and executioner."

—Principal Snyder, "School Hard"

Buffy: "I told one lie, I had one drink."
Giles: "And you nearly got devoured by a giant demon-snake. I think the words 'let that be a lesson' are a tad redundant at this juncture."

—"Reptile Boy"

Giles: "We should meet in front of the hospital at eight-thirty, sharp. I'll bring the weaponry."
Buffy: "And I'll bring the party mix."
Giles: (stern look) "Don't be late."
Buffy: "Giles, have I ever let you down?"
Giles: "Do you want me to answer that, or shall I just glare?"

—"The Dark Age"

Cordelia: "[Buffy's] like this superman. Shouldn't there be different rules for her?"
Willow: "Sure, in a fascist society."
Cordelia: "Right! Why can't we have one of those?"

—"Ted"

"Do you want me to wag my finger at you and tell you you acted rashly? You did, and I can. But I know you loved [Angel], and he has proven more than once that he loved you. You couldn't have known what would happen. The coming months are going to be very hard—I suspect on all of us. But if you're looking for guilt, Buffy, I'm not your man. All you will have from me is my support . . . and my respect."

—Giles, "Innocence"

"You know what? I don't care. I don't care. I don't care what your friends think of me—or you for that matter—because you put me through the wringer, Buffy. I mean it. And I've had schnapps!"

—Joyce, "Dead Man's Party"

Xander: "What a burn. Buff's mom was just starting to accept the Slayer thing. Now she's going to be double-freaked."

Willow: "Makes me glad my mother doesn't know about my extracurricular activities. Or my curricular activities. Or, you know, the fact of my activeness in general . . ."

—"Gingerbread"

"This is not a good town. How many of us have lost someone who just . . . disappeared, or got skinned, or suffered 'neck rupture'? And how many of us have been too afraid to speak out? I was supposed to lead us in a moment of silence. But silence is this town's disease. For too long, it's been plagued by unnatural evils. It's not our town anymore. It belongs to the monsters, to the witches and Slayers. I say it's time for the grown-ups to take Sunnydale back. I say we start by finding the people who did this and making them pay."

—Joyce, "Gingerbread"

"You earned this, you toyed with unnatural forces. . . . Buffy, what kind of mother would I be if I didn't punish you?"

—Joyce, "Gingerbread"

Wesley: "Are you not used to being given orders?"
Buffy: "Giles always says 'please' when he sends me on a mission. And afterwards, he gives me a cookie."

—"Bad Girls"

"If you want to criticize my methods, fine. But you can keep your snide remarks to yourself, and while you're at it, stop criticizing my methods!"

—Giles to Wesley, "Bad Girls"

Wesley: "[Buffy] cannot leave Sunnydale.
I forbid it."

Giles: "Oh, yes. That should settle it."

—"Choices"

"Of the two people here, which is the boss of me?"

—Firm Willow, "Choices"

Buffy: "I was. Studying. At the library. All night . . .
all Saturday night. Okay, you know what?
I'm an adult. It's none of your business
where I was."

Giles: "I'm sincerely glad to hear that."

—"The Harsh Light of Day"

"I walked by your guidance counselor's office one
time: A bunch of you were sitting there, waiting to
be . . . shepherded, to be guided. You and the other
problems, glassy-eyed, slack-jawed . . . I remember it
smelled like dead flowers. Like decay. And it hit me,
yes, that's what it is; the hope of our nation's future is
a bunch of mulch."

—Principal Snyder, "Restless"

Buffy: (on the Council) "They're coming here?
Now? Why do they have to come here?"

Xander: "Yeah, don't they have phones? 'Hallo,
Buffy, here's some stuff we know, pip
pip.'"

—"Checkpoint"

"They're all right when it comes to the rough stuff—a little ham-handed but they get it done. But this stuff, bureaucracy, pulling political strings, paperwork . . . this is where they're the best in the world. They can kill you with a stroke of the pen. Poncy buggers."

—**Giles, on the Council, "Checkpoint"**

"Are you sure they're English? I thought English people were gentler than normal people."

—**Tara, "Checkpoint"**

"You're Watchers. And without a Slayer you're pretty much just watching Masterpiece Theatre. You can't stop Glory. You can't do anything with the information you have on her except publish it in 'Everyone Thinks We're Insano's Home Journal.'"

—**Buffy, "Checkpoint"**

Xander: "Excuse me. Who made you the boss of the group?"

Anya: "You did."

Tara: "You said, 'Willow should be boss.'"

Anya: "And then you said, 'Let's vote,' and it was unanimous."

Tara: "You made her that little plaque that said, 'Boss of us,' you put on the sparkles—"

Xander: "Valid points, all."

—**"Bargaining, Part One"**

KN⊙WLEDGE

Xander: "Willow! You're so very much the person I wanted to see. You know, I kind of had a problem with the math?

Willow: "Which part?"

Xander: "The math."

    —"Welcome to the Hellmouth"

Willow: "Do you have *Theories in Trig*? You should check it out."

Xander: "Check it out?"

Willow: "From the library. Where the books live."

    —"Welcome to the Hellmouth."

Buffy: "See, a school has students, and they check out books, and then they learn things."

Giles: "I was beginning to suspect that was just a myth."

        —"Never Kill a Boy on the First Date"

Willow: "We have to go with Giles. He could get in trouble."

Xander: "He'll be fine. He's like Superlibrarian. Everyone forgets, Willow, that knowledge is the ultimate weapon."

—**"Never Kill a Boy on the First Date"**

Xander: "Buffy, this is not just about looking at a bunch of animals. This is about **not being in class**."

Buffy: "You're right. Suddenly the animals look shiny and new."

—**Re: the class trip to the zoo, "The Pack"**

Xander: "Why do I need to learn this?"

Willow: "'Cause otherwise you'll flunk math."

Xander: "Now explain the part where that's a bad thing."

Willow: "You remember: You fail math, you flunk out of school, you end up being the guy at the pizza place that sweeps the floor and says, 'Hey kids, where's the cool parties this weekend?'"

—**"The Pack"**

Willow: "How is it you always know this stuff? You always know what's going on—I never know what's going on."

Giles: "Yes, well, you weren't here from midnight to six researching it."

—**"Angel"**

Jenny: "You here again? You kids really dig on the library, don't you?"

Buffy: "We're literary."

Xander: "To read is makes our speaking English good."

—**"I Robot, You Jane"**

Jenny: "Honestly, what is it about them that bothers you so much?"

Giles: "The smell."

Jenny: "Computers don't smell, Rupert."

Giles: "I know. Smell is the most powerful memory trigger there is. A certain flower or a whiff of smoke can bring up experiences long forgotten. Books smell—musty and rich. Knowledge gained from a computer has no texture, no context. It's there and then it's gone. If it's to last, the getting of knowledge should be tangible. It should be smelly."

—**"I Robot, You Jane"**

The Master: "You were destined to die! It was written!"
Buffy: "What can I say? I flunked the written."

—**"Prophecy Girl"**

Xander: "I think the exchange student program is cool. I do. It's the beautiful melding of two cultures."
Buffy: "Have you ever **done** an exchange program?"
Xander: "My dad tried to sell me to some Armenians once, does that count?"

—**"Inca Mummy Girl"**

"You know what's so cool about college? The diversity. You've got the rich people and you've got . . . all the other people."

—**Cordelia, "Reptile Boy"**

"Well, evil just compounds evil, doesn't it? First I'm sentenced to a computer tutorial on Saturday, now I have to read some computer book. They have books about computers? Isn't that the point of computers, to *replace* books?"

—**Cordelia, "The Dark Age"**

Cordelia: "School on a Saturday? That throws off my internal clock."

Xander: "When are we going to have to use computers in real life, anyway?"

Jenny: "Let's see, there's home, school, work, games—"

Xander: "Computers are on the way out. I think paper is about to make a big comeback."

Willow: "And the abacus."

—**"The Dark Age"**

Willow: "And here we have the cafeteria, where we were mauled by snakes . . ."

Xander: "This is the spot where Angel tried to kill Willow."

Willow: "Over there in the lounge is where Spike and his gang nearly massacred us all on parent-teacher night. Oh, and up those stairs, I was sucked into a muddy grave . . ."

Xander: "They say young people don't learn anything in high school nowadays, but I've learned to be afraid."

—**Giving the guided tour to the new Slayer in town, "Faith, Hope & Trick"**

Joyce: "You should be at a good old-fashioned college, with keg parties and boys. Not here, with Hellmouths and vampires."

Buffy: "Not really seeing a huge distinction there . . ."

—**"Lovers Walk"**

"Is the world ending? I have to research a paper on Bosnia for tomorrow, but if the world's ending, I'm not gonna bother."

—**Cordelia, "Helpless"**

"I'm so overwhelmed. I got in! To colleges. Real live colleges! And now they're wooing me. They're pitching woo!"

—**Willow, "Bad Girls"**

Giles: "This is the SATs, Buffy, not connect-the-dots. Please pay attention. A low score could seriously harm your chances of getting into college."

Buffy: "Oh, that takes the pressure right off."

Giles: "This isn't supposed to be easy, you know. It's a rite of passage."

Buffy: "Is it too late to join a tribe where they just pierce something, or cut something off?"

—**"Choices"**

Buffy: "I can't believe you got into Oxford."

Oz: "You're into some deep academia there."

Buffy: "That's where they make Gileses!"

Willow: "I know! I could learn and have scones!"

—**"Choices"**

"Congratulations to the class of 1999. You've all proved more or less adequate. This is a time for celebration, so sit still and be quiet."

—**Principal Snyder, "Graduation Day, Part Two"**

Buffy: " 'Introduction to the Modern Novel.' I'm guessing I'd probably have to **read** the modern novel."

Willow: "Maybe more than one."

Buffy: "I like books. I just don't wanna take too much. Do they have 'Introduction to the Modern Blurb'?"

—**"The Freshman"**

"In high school, knowledge was pretty much frowned upon. You really had to work to learn anything. But here, I mean, the energy, the collective intelligence—it's like the force, this penetrating force; I can feel my mind just opening up, you know, letting the place just thrust into it and . . . spurt knowledge . . . into . . . That sentence ended up in a different place than it started out in."

—**Willow, "The Freshman"**

Willow: "Professor Walsh is supposed to be great. She's like world renowned."

Buffy: "How do you get renowned? Do you have to be nowned first?"

Willow: "Yes, first there is the painful nowning process."

—"The Freshman"

Willow: "Guess Ms. Walsh isn't so ogre-y after all."

Buffy: "Except now she wants me to lead a discussion group next class. Which means more work, right? Shouldn't she have a better reward system? Like a cookie? Or maybe a little toy, like at the dentist?"

—"Wild at Heart"

Willow: "Boy, that was an exciting class, huh?"

Buffy: "Oh, yeah."

Willow: "And that last twenty minutes—it was a revelation. Just laid out everything we needed to know for the final. I'd hate to have missed that."

Buffy: "Just tell me I didn't snore."

Willow: "You were very discreet. Minimal drool."

—"Hush"

"Drama class is just . . . I think they're not doing things in the proper way, and now I'm in a play, and my whole family's here, and why is there a cowboy in *Death of a Salesman,* anyway?"

—Willow, "Restless"

"I'm starting to think this 'working hard' is hard work. I thought it was gonna be more like in the movies. You know, inspirational music and a montage: me sharpening pencils, reading, writing, falling asleep on a big pile of books with my glasses all crooked, because in the montage I have glasses. Real life is so slow, and it hurts my occipital lobe."

—Buffy, "Out of My Mind"

"Why do people who don't go to college always refer to everything outside of college as the 'real world'? Like college is some imaginary realm with elves and witches and . . . Huh."

—Willow, "Tough Love"

"[Your homeroom teacher] responded to Buffybot because a robot is predictable, boring . . . a perfect teacher's pet. That's all schools are, you know, factories spewing mindless little automatons—" (quickly) "—who go on to be very productive and valuable members of society. And you should go. Because Buffy would want you to."

—Spike to Dawn, "Bargaining, Part One"

"You could still drop out. Only nerds finish school."
—Buffy to Dawn, "Lessons"

"Well, I better get to work. Got to start deadening young minds."

—Principal Wood, "Lessons"

Buffy: "Dawn—"
Dawn: "I know: You never see it coming. The stake is not the power. *To Serve Man* is a cookbook. I love you. Go away."

—"Lessons"

"I know high school can be frustrating. But if you just get through it, then you can go to college or join the French Foreign Legion or anything you want."

—Buffy, "Help"

"I almost forgot, somehow. I almost forgot how much high school hurts."

—Buffy, "Help"

"It's hard to do homework if you think you're about to die."

—Buffy, on something she knows a thing or two about, "Help"

THE BİG BAD

"I have waited. For three score years I have waited. While you come and go I have been stuck here," (voice raising) "here, in a house of **worship**. My ascension is almost at hand. Pray that when it comes . . . I'm in a better mood."

> **—The Master to Darla, "The Harvest"**

" Hold on—you've got something in your eye."

> **—The Master, as he jabs his finger into a minion's eye, "The Harvest"**

Giles: "Now, I do want to make sure I've got this right. This witch is casting horrible, disfiguring spells so that she can be a cheerleader."

Buffy: "Your point being?"

Giles: "Priorities. Really, if I had the power of the black mass I'd set my sights a little higher than making the pep squad."

> **—"The Witch"**

Buffy: "So I'm an undead monster who can shave with his hand—how many things am I afraid of?"

Giles: "Not many. And not substitute teachers, as a rule."

—Re: Natalie French, "Teacher's Pet"

"You know, I really felt bad for you. You've suffered. But there's one thing I didn't factor into all this. You're a thundering loony."

—Buffy to Marcie, the invisible girl, "Out of Mind, Out of Sight"

Absalom: "Your day is done, girl. I'll grind you into a sticky paste. And I'll hear you beg before I smash in your face."

Buffy: "So, are you gonna kill me? Or are you just making small talk?"

—"When She Was Bad"

"You know, just when you think you've seen it all, along comes a worm guy."

—Xander, "What's My Line? Part Two"

Giles: "Lyle Gorch. The other one is his brother Tector. They're from Abeline. Made their reputation massacring a Mexican village in 1886."

Buffy: "Friendly little demons . . ."

Giles: "No, that was *before* they became vampires."

—**"Bad Eggs"**

Giles: "[The Judge's] touch can literally burn the humanity out of you. A true creature of evil can survive the process. No human ever has."

Xander: "So what's the problem? We send Cordy to fight this guy and we go for pizza."

—**"Surprise"**

"Humans don't fight back. **Humans don't fight back.** *THAT'S HOW THIS WORKS!!*"

—**Ken, "Anne"**

"You've got guts. I think I'd like to split you open and play with them."

—**Ken to Buffy, "Anne"**

Mr. Trick: "You and me, girl. There's high times ahead."

Buffy: "They never just leave. They always gotta say something . . ."

—**"Band Candy"**

Angel: "Lagos?"

Buffy: "Yeah, he's some kind of demon looking for an all-powerful thingimibob, and I've got to stop him before unholy havoc's unleashed, and it's another Tuesday night in Sunnydale."

—**"Revelations"**

The First: "You think you can fight me. I'm not a demon, little girl. I'm something you can't conceive. The first evil. Beyond sin, beyond death . . . I am the thing the darkness fears. You will never see me, but I am everywhere. Every being, every thought, every drop of hate—"

Buffy: "I get it. *You're evil.* Do we have to chat about it all day?"

—**"Amends"**

"With any luck, [the Slayers]'ll kill each other. And then everyone's a winner. Everyone, of course, being me."

—**The Mayor, "Bad Girls"**

Faith: "Thanks, sugar daddy."

Mayor: "Oh! Faith. I don't find that sort of thing amusing. I'm a family man. Now. Let's kill your little friend."

—**"Doppelgangland"**

Anya: "I swear, I'm just trying to find my necklace."

Willow: "Did you try looking inside the sofa in HELL?"

—**Alternate realities are neat, "Doppelgangland"**

Buffy: "I don't know what that stupid Mayor was on about, talking about our relationship like he knows anything about us."

Angel: "Well, he's evil."

—**"Choices"**

"My God, what a feeling. The power of these creatures . . . it suffuses my being. I can feel the changes begin. My organs shifting, merging, making ready for the Ascension. . . . Plus, these babies are high in fiber, and what's the fun of becoming an immortal demon if you're not regular, am I right?"

—**The Mayor thinks Gavrok spiders are nutritious *and* delicious, "Graduation Day, Part One"**

Xander: "Some friends of Buffy's played a funny joke; they took her stuff, and now she wants us to help get it back from her friends who sleep all day and have no tans."

Willow: "Oh, those friends."

Oz: "They're funny guys."

—**The gang tries to be subtle in public, The Freshman**

"Giles, she has parts that keep growing after they're detached. She irons her jeans! She's evil!"

—Buffy, on Kathy, "The Freshman"

"Harmony's a vampire? She must be dying without a reflection."

—Buffy, "The Harsh Light of Day"

"Hey, I don't have a pulse. Can we eat a doctor and get a stethoscope so I can hear my heart not beating?"

—Harmony, "The Harsh Light of Day"

Giles: "Don't taunt the fear demon."
Xander: "Why? Can he hurt me?"
Giles: "No, it's just . . . tacky."

—"Fear, Itself"

"[Demons are] just animals, man. Plain and simple. Granted, a little rarer than the ones you grew up with on that little farm in Smallville, but . . ."

—Forrest to Riley, "Doomed"

Giles: "Listen, about Fyarl demons . . . do I—do I have any special powers? Setting things on fire with my sizzling eye beams?"

Spike: "Oh, yeah. You got a power. The ability to shoot out huge jets of paralyzing mucus."

Giles: "What? Mucus?"

Spike: "Paralyzing mucus: shoots out the nose, sets up fast. Hard as a rock. Pretty good in a fight."

Giles: "You're making this up."

Spike: "Maybe. But, hey, you feel a sneeze coming on, you warn me."

—"A New Man"

Giles: "I . . . I think I'm changing. It's like a . . . a mindless need to destroy things. Anger. Rage."

Spike: "Good times. Go with it."

—"A New Man"

Spike: "How're you feeling, mate?"

Giles: "Like snapping necks until everyone's dead."

Spike: "Now *that* sounds like a Fyarl demon."

—"A New Man"

Buffy: "Think about it. Who better to bring a bunch of demon types together than someone who's made up of a bunch of demon types?"

Tara: "So, he's, um, bridging the gap between the races?"

Willow: "Huh. Like Martin Luther King. But probably a lot less eloquent . . . and with the . . . evil . . . so, different than Martin Luther King."

   —Re: Adam, "Where the Wild Things Are"

Buffy: "I could barely fight [Adam]. It sounded like Maggie designed him to be the ultimate warrior. He's smart, and fast. . . . He gave the commando guys the slip with no problem."

Willow: "There's got to be a flaw—"

Buffy: "I'd say the part where he's pure evil and kills randomly was an oversight . . ."

   —"Goodbye, Iowa"

"Ask around, look it up. 'Slayer comma the'?"—Buffy

"Don't warn the tadpoles!"—Willow

"I'm sick of being the guy who eats the insects and gets the funny syphilis!"—Xander

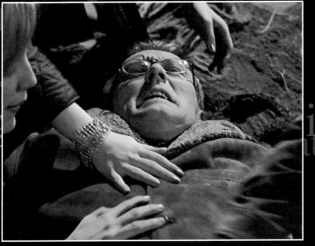

"I'm great with the pacing and the saying of 'hmmm,' and 'ahhhhhh,' and 'good Lord!'"—Giles

"He wears lifts, you know." —Spike, re: Angel

"This is all about me! Me! Me! Me!"—Cordelia

"Am I the good Slayer now?"—Faith

"I could *so* save the world if somebody handed me superpowers."—Dawn

"You've really mastered the single entendre."—Oz

"I'm not sure you should say 'sex poodle' in your vows."—Tara

"This is the crack team that foils my every plan? I am deeply shamed."—Spike

"We are as gods!"—Andrew

"So . . . what do you wanna do tomorrow?"
—Buffy

Adam: "You feel smothered. Trapped like an animal, pure in its ferocity, unable to actualize the urges within . . . clinging to one truth like a flame struggling to burn within an enclosed glass . . . that a beast this powerful cannot be contained. Inevitably it will break free and savage the land again. . . . I will make you whole again. Make you savage."

Spike: "Wow. I mean, yeah. I get why the demons all fall in line with you. You're like Tony Robbins if he was a big, scary Frankenstein-looking . . . You're exactly like Tony Robbins."

—**"The Yoko Factor"**

Harmony: "So, Slayer . . . At last we meet."
Buffy: "We've met, Harmony, you halfwit."
—**"Real Me"**

"I saw Buffy patrolling just now. With a stake! She won't give up till she's killed me to death. That's why I'm on the lam. I'm totally her archnemesis."
—**Harmony, "Out of My Mind"**

Giles: "You didn't give me much to go on. She looks human, so the mug shots aren't any use. . . . You can't be a bit more specific about what she was like?"

Buffy: "She was kind of like . . . well, she was kind of like Cordelia, actually. If she were on steroids. That were on steroids." (not helpful) "I'm pretty sure she dyes her hair."

—Re: Glory, "Family"

Drusilla: "The King of Cups expects a picnic, but this is not his birthday."

Darla: (what?) "Good . . . point."

—"Fool for Love"

Giles: "All we have to worry about is her being immortal, invulnerable, and on the constant brink of insanity."

Xander: "A *crazy* hellgod? And the fun just keeps on leaving."

—"Blood Ties"

Spike: "You're never gonna get your sodding Key, because you might be strong, but in our world, you're an idiot."

Glory: "Stop it! I am a god."

Spike: "The god of what? Bad home perms?"

—"Intervention"

"Lot of sucky things in this dimension. Bubble baths? Not one of 'em, know what I mean?"

—Glory, "Tough Love"

Tara: "I thought vengeance demons only punished men who wronged women."

Halfrek: "No, that was just Anya's little *raison d'être*. Most of us try to be a bit more well-rounded. . . . Oh, and we actually prefer 'justice demon.' FYI."

—"Older and Far Away"

"How could [Warren] do that to me? He promised we'd be together. He was just using me. He never really loved . . . hanging out with us."

—Andrew, "Seeing Red"

"That guy's been looking at me. I think he wants to make me his butt monkey."

—Jonathan on prison life, "Villains"

Andrew: "[Warren's] just coming up with a plan. Like in *War Games*, remember? That decoder Matthew Broderick used?"

Jonathan: "Oh, yeah. That was rad. The one he made from the scissors and the tape recorder?"

Andrew: "I miss 'Ferris' Matthew. 'Broadway' Matthew—I find him cold."

—"Villains"

"You think your Li'l Witch buddy's gonna stop with us? You saw her! She's a truck-driving magic mama. We've got maybe seconds before Darth Rosenberg grinds everybody into Jawa-burgers, and not one of you bunch has the midiclorians to stop her."

—Andrew on evil Willow, "Two to Go"

"'From beneath you it devours.' It's not the friendliest jingle, is it? It's no 'I like Ike' or 'Milk: It does a body good.'"

—Xander, "Help"

Jonathan: "We should have stayed in Mexico."
Andrew: "I didn't like it there. Everyone spoke Mexico-an."

—"Conversations with Dead People"

"*We* find it, *we* alert the Slayer, *we* help her destroy it, *we* save Sunnydale . . . then we join her gang and possibly hang out at her house."

—Andrew: a man with a plan, "Conversations with Dead People"

Jonathan: "I miss my friends. I miss my enemies. I miss the people I talked to every day. And I miss the people who never knew I existed. I miss 'em all. I want to talk to them, ya know? I wanna find out how they're doing. I want to know what's going on in their lives."

Andrew: "Yeah? Well, you know what? They don't want to talk to you. All those people you just mentioned—not one of them's sitting around going, 'I wonder what Jonathan's up to right now.' Not one of them cares about you."

Jonathan: "Well, I still care about them. That's why I'm here."

> —**"Conversations with Dead People"**

Warren/The First: "Hey, you know the rules. I can't take corporeal form."

Andrew: "Cool."

Warren: "Yeah. It's pretty bitchin'. I'm like Obi-Wan."

Andrew: "Or Patrick Swayze . . ."

> —**"Never Leave Me"**

Rona: "Um . . . why's that guy tied to a chair?"

Xander: "The question you'll soon be asking is why isn't he gagged?"

> —**Re: Andrew, "Showtime"**

Beljoxa's Eye: "The Eye sees not the future. Only the truths of now and before."

Anya: "Yes! We all have that! It's called memory!"

—Not so much with the helpful, "Showtime"

"[Andrew's] not evil, but when he gets close to it he picks up its flavor like a mushroom or something."

—Buffy, "Potential"

Andrew: "It's not fair. Spike just killed people and he gets to go."

Buffy: "Spike didn't have free will. You did."

Andrew: "Oh, I hate my free will."

—"Potential"

Buffy: "This is Andrew. He's our . . . actually, he's our hostage."

Andrew: "I like to think of myself more as a"—air quotes—"'guest-age.'"

—"Get It Done"

"He was evil, people died, now he bakes. It's a thing."

—Buffy, re: Andrew, "Get It Done"

"He's a breath of fresh air, isn't he? Thank God I don't breathe."

—Spike, re: Andrew, "Touched"

The First: "I want to feel. I want to put my hands around an innocent neck and feel it crack. I want to bite off a young girl's face and feel the skin and gristle slither down my throat."

Caleb: "Now that is truly poetical."

—"Touched"

"You know, you really should watch your language. Someone who didn't know you might think you were a woman-hating prick."

—Buffy to Caleb, "Touched"

FASHION

"Willow! Nice dress. Good to know you've seen the softer side of Sears."

— **Cordelia, "Welcome to the Hellmouth"**

(Buffy is in her bedroom, in the agony of outfit choosage, getting ready to go out. She has two: one scanty, the other somewhat plain. She holds them alternately in front of her, looking in the mirror.)
(holding up one) "Hi! I'm an enormous slut!"
(the other) "Hi! Would you like a copy of the *Watchtower*?"

— **Buffy, "Welcome to the Hellmouth"**

Giles: "A Slayer should be able to see vampires. Without looking, without thinking. Can you tell me if there's a vampire in this building?"

Buffy: "There's one."

Giles: "But you don't know—"

Buffy: "Oh, please. Look at his jacket. He's got the sleeves rolled up. And the shirt . . . Deal with that outfit for a moment."

— **"Welcome to the Hellmouth"**

Buffy: "Okay. Do I want to appear shy, coy, and naive, or do I go unrestrained, insatiable, and aggressive?"

Xander: "You know, Owen is a little homespun. He probably doesn't like that overly assertive look." (looking in her closet) "Hey, here's something. A nice, comfy overcoat. And this ski cap. The earflaps will bring out your eyes."

—"Never Kill a Boy on the First Date"

"I don't know what everyone's talking about; that outfit doesn't make you look like a hooker."

—Xander to Cordelia, "Angel"

Darla: "Do you know what the saddest thing in the world is?"

Buffy: "Bad hair on top of that outfit?"

—Catfight in progress, "Angel"

Jenny: "You really are an old-fashioned boy, aren't you?"

Giles: "Well, it's true I don't dangle a corkscrew from my ear . . ."

Jenny: "That's not where it dangles."

— "I Robot, You Jane"

Giles: "[Buffy] was only grounded for a moment.
Still, if you'd been anyone but the Slayer . . ."

Buffy: "Tell me the truth. How's my hair?"

—Priorities, "I Robot, You Jane"

Giles: "I'm sorry, there's something . . . your hair.
Seems a bit odd."

Cordelia: "There's something wrong with my hair?
Oh, my God." (She hurries off.)

Giles: "Xander was right. Works like a charm."

—"The Puppet Show"

"I am, of course, having my dress specially made.
Off-the-rack gives me hives."

—Cordelia, "Out of Mind, Out of Sight"

Cordelia: "Willow! Hi. I like your outfit."

Willow: "No, you don't."

Cordelia: "No, I really don't. But I need a favor."

—"Prophecy Girl"

The Master: "You . . . are dead."

Buffy: "I may be dead, but I'm still pretty. Which
is more than I can say for you."

—"Prophecy Girl"

"What an ordeal. And you know the worst part: It stays with you forever. No matter what they tell you, none of that rust and blood and grime comes out. You can dry-clean till judgment day; you're living with those stains."

—Cordelia names the downside to being involved in a ritual sacrifice, "When She Was Bad"

Willow: "It's a celebration of cultures. There's lots of dress-up alternatives."

Xander: "And a corresponding equal number of mocking alternatives, all aimed at me."

Willow: "Bavarians are cool."

Xander: "No hats with feathers, no ruffled shirts, and *definitely* no lederhosen. They make my calves look fat."

—Xander is wary of dressing up for the cultural celebration dance, "Inca Mummy Girl"

"What kind of girl travels with a mummified corpse . . . and doesn't even pack a lipstick?"

—Buffy questions Ampata's grooming practices, "Inca Mummy Girl"

"Buffy. Love your hair. It just *screams* street urchin."

—Cordelia catches Buffy at an off moment, "Halloween"

"You know, Giles, I realize the Henry Higgins bit may have been the mod look for your generation, but a lot has happened since then. Like the twentieth century, for example."

> **—Buffy, re: Giles's attempts to set himself apart from the students sartorially, "The Dark Age"**

Buffy: "Don't you understand? This is so important!"

Joyce: "It's an outfit. An outfit that you may never buy."

Buffy: "But . . . I looked good in it!"

Joyce: "You looked like a streetwalker!"

Buffy: "But a **thin** streetwalker!" (beat) "That's probably not gonna be the winning argument, is it?"

Joyce: "You're just too young to wear that."

Buffy: "I'm gonna be too young to wear that till I'm too old to wear that."

Joyce: "That's the plan . . ."

> **—"Bad Eggs"**

"It's a clothes fluke, and that's what it is, and there'll *be* no more fluking!"

> **—Xander, re: pre-Homecoming Willow kissage, "Homecoming"**

Cordelia: "That thing had good taste. I mean, he chucked Xander and went right for the formal wear."

Xander: "That's right. And he left behind his copy of Monster's Wear Daily."

—Attack of the devil dog fashionistas, "Choices"

Willow: "Not too short. Medium. And it had this wild sort of fringy stuff on the arms—"

Giles: "What's this? A demon?"

Buffy: "A prom dress that Will was thinking about buying. Can't you ever get your mind out of the Hellmouth?"

—"Choices"

Xander: "I like the blue [robe]. Has more dignity."

Cordelia: "Dignity? You? In relation to clothes? I'm awash in a sea of confusion."

—"Graduation Day, Part One"

Buffy: "I thought people in college were supposed to get smarter."

Sunday: "I think you had a lot of misconceptions about college. Like that anyone would be caught dead wearing **that**."

—"The Freshman"

Sunday: "Those jeans with the little patches?"
Dav: "I hear they're coming back."
Sunday: "Not if I kill every single person who wears them."

—**"The Freshman"**

Dav: "Does this sweater make me look fat?"
Sunday: "No, the fact that you're fat makes you look fat. The sweater makes you look purple."

—**"The Freshman"**

"Ugh! Cotton! Could a fabric be more annoyingly pedestrian?"

—**Glory, "Blood Ties"**

Buffy: "It'll fit."
Xander: "Aw, man. What if it doesn't? What if I can't wear my cummerbund and the whole world can see the place where my pants meet my shirt? That can't happen, Buffy! I must wear das cummerbund!"

—**"Hell's Bells"**

Willow: "I'll say this for the Y chromosome: Looks good in a tux."
Xander: "Your double Xs aren't doing so bad there either."

—**"Hell's Bells"**

"It's a good thing I realized I was gay. 'Cause otherwise, hey, you, me, and formal wear . . ."

—Willow lets Xander know that there'll be no more fluking, "Hell's Bells"

"You're unconscionably spiffy."

—Buffy, re: Xander's "middle management" ensemble, "Lessons"

"First, you said you were going to the library. Second, you don't go on a date without informing me first. And third, Anna Nicole Smith thinks you look tacky."

—Buffy to Dawn, "Him"

The First: "Do you think I'm God?"

Caleb: "I surely do not. I'm beyond concepts like that."

The First: "But you still wear the outfit . . ."

Caleb: "Man can't turn his back on what he come from. Besides, black is slimming. Everyone knows that."

—A fashion-forward preacher man, "Dirty Girls"

F·O·OD

Buffy: "Hot-dog surprise . . . be still my heart."
Willow: "Call me old-fashioned, I don't want any
more surprises in my hot dogs . . ."
—**Re: cafeteria food, "Teacher's Pet"**

Xander: "Has anyone given any
thought to what this green
stuff is?"
Buffy: "I'm avoiding the subject."
Xander: "I think it's kale. Or possibly
string cheese."
—**And yet more yummy cafeteria
food, "Never Kill a Boy on the
First Date"**

"I ate a pig? Was he cooked and
called bacon or . . . oh, my God. Ate
a pig. I mean, the whole trichinosis
issue aside, yuck."
—**Xander thinks about going
veg after some hyena possession,
"The Pack"**

"You're Amish, you won't fight back because you're
Amish . . . I mock you with my ice cream cone,
Amish guy . . ."

> **—Xander chooses his weapon,
> "When She Was Bad"**

"It's a delicious, golden, spongy cake filled with a
delightful, white creamy substance of goodness. And
the exciting part is, they have no ingredients that a
human can pronounce. So they don't leave you with
that heavy, **food** feeling in your stomach."

> **—Xander, re: the joys of Twinkies,
> "Inca Mummy Girl"**

"The monkey is the only cookie animal that gets to
wear clothes, you know that? So I'm wondering, do
the other cookie animals feel sort of ripped? Like, is
the hippo going, 'Man, where are my pants? I have
my hippo dignity . . .'"

> **—Oz, "What's My Line? Part Two"**

"I'm eating this banana. Lunchtime be damned!"

> **—Willow rebels, "Doppelgangland"**

Xander: "Aren't you supposed to be drinking tea,
anyway?"

Giles: "Tea is soothing. I wish to be tense."

> **—"Graduation Day, Part Two"**

Buffy: "There is no problem that cannot be solved by chocolate."

Willow: "I think I'm gonna barf."

Buffy: "Except that."

—**"Fear, Itself"**

"That's the great thing about beer. Makes all men the same."

—**Jack, "Beer Bad"**

"I like pancakes. They're stackable. And waffles, 'cause you could put stuff in the little holes if you wanted to."

—**Buffy, "A New Man"**

Xander: "You're looking at the new local distributor for Boost Bars. The 'natural food bar that provides a nutritional energy boost for active, health-conscious people.' Want one?"

Willow: "Nah, thanks. Those things usually taste kinda tasteless. And they leave a bad aftertasteless taste."

—**"The I in Team"**

Xander: "Dinner is served! My very own recipe."

Willow: "You pushed the button on the microwave marked 'popcorn'?"

Xander: "Actually, I pushed 'defrost.' But Joyce was there in the clinch."

—**"Restless"**

"Mmm. Artificial cheese-flavored powder. Nature's perfect food."

—**Buffy, "Crush"**

"Look at these tiny grain patties—they're woven! That's craftsmanship."

—**Anya marvels at the wonder of Chex mix, "I Was Made to Love You"**

Buffy: "Chicken salad?"

Willow: "Right here."

Buffy: "Eggplant, that's me. And, what is this, peanut butter and . . . eew, *salami*—Dawn?"

Dawn: "Yeah, like eggplant is normal. It's what—half egg, half plant? 'Cause that's just unnatural."

—**"Tough Love"**

"Hey. I think Anya's gonna try to cook. Wanna come watch the tears and recriminations?"

—**Dawn, "Spiral"**

Giles: "M'Fashnik. Oh."

Dawn: "Aha! Like 'Mmm, Cookies.'"

Giles: "No, quite different, actually."

—Giles explains the subtle difference between demons and baked goods, "Flooded"

Buffy: "Here you go. One Medley Meal. Plus I double-sized your fries . . . and cut way back on the cat."

Xander: "Kmmmph?"

Buffy: "I'm probably kidding."

—"Doublemeat Palace"

Phillip: "Every burger at every Doublemeat Palace is the same. People don't like variation."

Buffy: "Got it. Variety is the spice of bad."

—"Doublemeat Palace"

"It's people! The Doublemeat Medley is *people*!!! The beefy layer is definitely people! Probably not the chicken-y part! But who knows! WHO KNOWS?!"

—Buffy, "Doublemeat Palace"

Buffy: "You gotta eat! I made cereal!"

Xander: "How exactly do you 'make' cereal?"

Buffy: "You put the box near the milk. I saw it on the food channel."

—"Lessons"

Dawn: "Let's go downstairs and I'll make you a nice cup of tea."

Buffy: "I hate tea."

Dawn: "Me too. It's the gesture. Come on. . . . You know we can never tell Giles about the tea thing, right?"

—**"Beneath You"**

"Sunnydale: Come for the food, stay for the dismemberment."

—**Xander, "Beneath You"**

"Anchovies, anchovies, you're so delicious / I love you more than all other fishes."

—**An ode to the unsung fish, by Dawn, "Conversations with Dead People"**

Andrew: "You sure you don't wanna stop and pick up some burgers or something? You know, road-trip food—"

Spike: "It's not a road trip. It's a covert operation."

Andrew: "Right, right, gotcha." (beat) "I bet even covert operatives eat curly fries, they're really good." (awkward silence)

Spike: "Not as good as those onion blossom things."

Andrew: "I love those! It's an onion, yet it's a flower. I don't understand how such a thing is possible."

Spike: "See, the genius is, you soak it in ice water for an hour so it holds its shape, then you deep-fry it root-side up for about five minutes."

Andrew: "Masterful."

Spike: "Yeah." (beat) "If you tell anyone we had this conversation, I'll bite you."

—"Empty Places"

Andrew: "It was pretty exciting. A whole grocery store, just abandoned. Food lying around everywhere. The produce was on its way to funky town, but the other stuff was just—"

Giles: "Oh for God's sake!"

Andrew: "Okay, I did a little looting, which is technically unethical, but these girls need to eat—"

Giles: "Andrew, things are getting very dire around here, and we've got more important things to worry about than—Ooh! Jaffa Cakes!"

—Priorities, check, "End of Days"

HOLIDAYS

Xander: "Halloween? I figured it would be a big old vamp 'scare-a-palooza.'"

Buffy: "Not according to Giles. He swears that tomorrow night is, like, dead for the un-dead. They stay in."

Xander: "Those wacky vampires. That's what I love about 'em. They just keep you guessing."

—**"Halloween"**

Buffy: "It wasn't exactly a perfect Thanksgiving."

Xander: "I don't know. It kinda seemed right to me. A bunch of anticipation, a big fight, and now we're all sleepy."

—**"Pangs"**

"Giles, if you want to get by in American society you have to learn our traditions. You're the patriarch. You have to host the festivities or it's all meaningless."

—**Buffy, "Pangs"**

Anya: "I love a ritual sacrifice."

Buffy: "It's not really one of those."

Anya: "To commemorate a past event, you kill and eat an animal. It's a ritual sacrifice. With pie."

—**"Pangs"**

Willow: "Buffy, earlier you agreed with me about Thanksgiving. It's a sham! It's all about death!"

Buffy: "It's a sham, but it's a sham with yams. A yam sham."

Willow: "You're not going to jokey-rhyme your way out of this one."

—**"Pangs"**

MONEY

Xander: "I bribed him."

Buffy: "How much?"

Xander: "Twenty-eight bucks. . . . Does the Council reimburse for that stuff?"

Giles: "Did you get a receipt?"

Xander: "Damn."

—**"Enemies"**

Anya: "Xander, you haven't been paying any attention to me tonight—just peddling those processed food bricks. I don't know why."

Xander: "Let me put it in a way you'll understand. . . . Sell bars, make money, take Anya nice places, buy pretty things."

Anya: "That does make sense."

—**"The I in Team"**

Xander: "Anya, the Shopkeepers Union of America called? They want me to tell you 'please go' just got replaced with 'have a nice day.'"

Anya: "I have their money. Who cares what kind of day they have?"

—**"No Place Like Home"**

"I'm thinking about buying something very expensive. Maybe an antelope."

—**Anya, "I Was Made to Love You"**

Buffybot: "Anya! How's your money?"

Anya: "Fine! Thank you for asking."

—**"Intervention"**

Willow: "I need help."

Anya: "I don't have any money."

Willow: "I don't want money!"

Anya: "Come in! Enjoy my personal space!"

—**"Same Time, Same Place"**

Hallie: "There's a revolution going on outside. That you're somewhat responsible for. Aren't you even the teeniest bit interested?"

Anya: "What's there to be interested in? The worker will overthrow the absolutism and lead the proletariat to a victorious communist revolution, resulting in socioeconomic paradise on Earth. It's common sense, really."

—"Selfless"

FEAR, ITSELF

"I laugh in the face of danger. Then I hide
till it goes away."
—Xander, "The Witch"

Willow: "I think dummies are cute.
You don't?"
Buffy: "They give me the wig.
Ever since I was little."
Willow: "What happened?"
Buffy: "I saw one. It gave me the
wig. There wasn't really a
story there."
—"The Puppet Show"

"Fear. It's a most wonderful thing. It is the
most powerful force in the human
world. Not love, not hate. Fear."
—The Master, "Nightmares"

"I don't like spiders, okay? Their furry bodies, their sticky webs—what do they need all those legs for, anyway? I'll tell you: for crawling across your face in the middle of the night."

—Willow, "Nightmares"

"I'm sorry, I'm unruffled by spiders. Now, if a bunch of Nazis crawled across my face . . ."

—Xander, "Nightmares"

"I'm sorry—staying calm may work fine for Locutus of the Borg here, but I'm freaked out and I plan to stay that way."

—Xander, "Prophecy Girl"

Angel: "I've seen this type before. They're children, making up bedtime stories about friendly vampires to comfort themselves in the dark."

Willow: "Is that so bad? The dark can get pretty dark, sometimes you need a story."

—"Lie to Me"

Cordelia: "What are we gonna do?"

Giles: "I'm leaning toward blind panic, myself."

—On Angel's defection, "Innocence"

Buffy: "Are you okay?"

Willow: "I'm fine. The shaking is a side effect of the fear."

—"The Zeppo"

Willow: "Hey, I eat danger for breakfast."

Xander: "But oddly enough she panics in the face of breakfast foods."

—**"Choices"**

"Buffy, this is all about fear. It's understandable, but you can't let it control you. Fear leads to anger. Anger leads to hate. Hate leads to anger . . . no, wait. . . . Fear leads to hate, hate leads to the dark side. . . . Hold on. . . . Hate . . . no . . . first you get the women, then you get the money, then you get . . . okay, forget that."

—**Xander, "The Freshman"**

Buffy: "Everybody grab a weapon. We've got to move."

Xander: "And storm the Initiative? Yeah . . . let's take on those suckers!"

Buffy: "I was more thinking that we'd hide."

Xander: "Oh, thank God."

—**"Goodbye, Iowa"**

"Oh, God. I'm terrified. I didn't think . . . I just figured **you** would be terrified and I would be sarcastic about it."

—**Anya to Andrew, re: imminent battle, "Chosen"**

WAR

"Now, we can do this the hard way, or . . . well, actually, there's just the hard way."
   —Buffy to Darla, "Welcome to the Hellmouth"

Giles: "Whatever you do, it's got to be sudden and swift—this beast is dangerous."

Buffy: "Well, your buddy Carlyle faced it, he's still around."

Giles: "Yes, in a straight jacket howling his innards out day and night."

Buffy: "Okay, Admiral, way to inspire the troops."
   —"Teacher's Pet"

Giles: "Two of the brethren were here. They came after me, but I was more than a match for them."

Buffy: "Meaning?"

Giles: "I hid."
   —"Never Kill a Boy on the First Date"

Spike: "Tell you what. As a personal favor from me to you, I'll make it quick. It won't hurt a bit."

Buffy: "Wrong. It's gonna hurt **a lot**."

—**"School Hard"**

"Some guy's attacking Buffy with a sword! Also, there's a really big snake."

—**Willow sums up the sitch, "Reptile Boy"**

Cordelia: "This is great. There's an unkillable demon in town, Angel's joined his team, and the Slayer is a basket case. I'd say we've hit bottom."

Xander: "I have a plan."

Cordelia: "Oh, no, here's a lower place."

—**"Innocence"**

Buffy: "Hey, Ken. Wanna see my impression of Gandhi?" (Ken looks blearily at her. She swings the club down on his head with horrible force. We hear a wet sound that comes from inside his head.)

Lily: (weakly) "Gandhi?"

Buffy: "Well, you know . . . if he was really pissed off."

—**"Anne"**

Faith:	"Nicely diverted, B.!"
Buffy:	"That wasn't diverting! That was fighting for my life, Miss Attention Span."
Faith:	"Hey, this isn't a Tupperware party. It's a little harder to plan."
Buffy:	"'The count of three' is not a plan. It's Sesame Street."

—**"Bad Girls"**

Faith:	"We *are* better. That's right. Better. People need us to survive. In the balance? Nobody's gonna cry over some random bystander who got caught in the crossfire."
Buffy:	"I am."

—**"Consequences"**

Giles:	"So, what's your plan?"
Buffy:	"I gotta have a plan? Really? I can't just be proactive with pep?"
Giles:	"You want to take the fight to them. I suggest the first step would be to find out what exactly they're up to."
Buffy:	"I actually knew that. I thought you meant a real specific plan, you know, with maps and stuff."

—**"Choices"**

"Actually, this isn't about you. Although I'm fond, don't get me wrong, of you. The other night, getting captured and all, facing off with Faith . . . things just got kind of clear. I mean, you've been fighting evil here for about three years, and I've been helping out some, and now we're supposed to be deciding what we wanna do with our lives, and I realized that's what I want to do. Fight evil. Help people. I think it's worth doing, and I don't think you do it 'cause you have to. It's a good fight, Buffy, and I want in."

—Willow, on her decision to stay in Sunnydale for college, "Choices"

Buffy: "Faith told me I'd have to play on his human weakness. That's the way I'm gonna get him."
Willow: "Faith told you? Was that before or after you put her in a coma?"
Buffy: "After."
Willow: "Oh."

—"Graduation Day, Part Two"

Xander: "You up for a little reconnaissance?"
Buffy: "You mean where we all paint and sculpt and stuff like that?"

—"The Freshman"

"The history of the world is not people making friends. You had better weapons, you massacred them, end of story!"

—Spike, fed up with political correctness, "Pangs"

"Okay, say this quake *was* a sign—a bad omen. And we just ignore it. There's gonna be some pretty red faces around here if the world comes to an end."

—**Buffy, "Doomed"**

"I'm going to the crime scene and see what I can find out. You guys research the Polgara demon—I want to know where it is. And when I find it, I'm going to make him pay for taking that kid's life. I'll make him die in ways he can't even imagine." (A beat. Then Buffy looks down at herself. Falters.) "That . . . probably would have sounded more commanding if I wasn't wearing my Yummy Sushi pyjamas."

—**Buffy, "Goodbye, Iowa"**

Xander: "So, here it is. The latest in state-of-the-art combat technology. I gotta say, it doesn't look that complicated."
Buffy: "So, can you repair it?"
Xander: "Sure. Just as soon as I get my master's degree in advanced *starship technology*."
Willow: "Well, why don't we experiment, then? You know, press some buttons, see what happens."
Xander: "It's called a 'Blaster,' Will. A word that tends to discourage experimentation. Now, if it was called 'The Orgasminator,' I'd be the first to try your basic button-press approach."

—**"This Year's Girl"**

Xander: (yelling) "HEY! Riley! What's the . . ." (hand gestures) ". . . all about?"

Riley: (five paces up ahead, sighs) "It means yell real loud so the vampires who don't know we're coming will have a sporting chance."

—**"Fool for Love"**

Giles: "Perhaps there's something in the Book of Tarnis, something we've missed that we can use against Glory."

Anya: "Piano!"

Xander: "Right. Piano. Because that's just what we used to kill that big demon that one time. No, wait. That was a rocket launcher."

Anya: "We should drop a piano on her. . . . It always works for that creepy cartoon rabbit when he's running from that nice man with the speech impediment."

Giles: "Yes, or perhaps we could paint a convincing fake tunnel on the side of a mountain."

—**"Spiral"**

Buffy: "Everybody ready?"

Xander: "You bet. Full of that good old Kamikaze spirit."

Giles: "Xander. Just because this can never work is no reason to be so negative."

—**Re: entering the belly of the beast, "Primeval"**

Colonel McNamara: "Who the hell do you people think you are?!? Infiltrating *my* base on *my* watch—issuing threats and brandishing weapons like, like . . ." (angrily rummages through Giles's bag) "What is this?" (embarrassed pause)

Willow: (small voice) ". . . Gourd."

Xander: ". . . Magic . . . gourd."

Giles: "It's less formidable out of context, you see . . ."

—"Primeval"

Xander: "Here's a handy rule: Don't waste your time with flashy tentacles just 'cause they're waving around trying to get attention. Go for the center—brain, heart, eyes. Everything's got eyes."

Dawn: "Except the Bringers."

Xander: "Except the Bringers."

—"Dirty Girls"

Buffy: "You guys are our safety net. This thing's a trap, we give the signal and you come in, guns blazing, after us."

Xander: "What's the signal?"

Buffy: "I'm thinking lots and lots of yelling."

—Buffy's got a plan, "Dirty Girls"

Buffy: "Caleb came looking for seconds."

Giles: "Good lord. Is he . . ."

Buffy: "Still able to make me see little cartoon birdies around my head? You betcha. The short lack of consciousness was nice, though. I feel rested."

—"Empty Places"

"We're all on death's doorstep, repeatedly ringing the bell, like maniacal Girl Scouts intent on making quota."

—Anya, "Touched"

Andrew: "We need supplies. And not just bandages and junk. These girls need stitches and pain killers . . ."

Anya: "And I could use a cookie. But I'm not making reckless wishes."

—"End of Days"

EVIL

Giles: "Dig a bit into the history of this place and you'll find there've been a steady stream of fairly odd occurrences. I believe this area is a center of mystical energy. Things gravitate toward it that you might not find elsewhere."

Buffy: "Like vampires."

Giles: "Like werewolves. Zombies. Succubi, incubi . . . everything you ever dreaded under your bed and told yourself couldn't be by the light of day."

Buffy: "What, did you send away for the Time Life series?"

Giles: "Uh, yes."

—"Welcome to the Hellmouth"

Giles: "The world is older than any of you know, and contrary to popular mythology, it did not begin as a paradise. For untold eons, demons walked the Earth, made it their home . . . their hell. In time they lost their purchase on this reality, and the way was made for the mortal animals. For Man. What remains of the Old Ones are vestiges: certain magicks, certain creatures . . ."

Buffy: "And vampires."

—"The Harvest"

"The books tell that the last demon to leave this reality fed off a human, mixed their blood. He was a human form possessed—infected—by the demon's soul. He bit another, and another, and another . . . and so they walk the earth, feeding. Killing some, mixing their blood with others to make more of their kind. Waiting for the animals to die out, and the Old Ones to return."

—Giles, "The Harvest"

"I don't like vampires. I'm gonna take a stand and say they're not good."

—Xander, "The Harvest"

"Well, that is the thrill of living on a Hellmouth—one has a veritable cornucopia of fiends, devils, and ghouls to engage—" (off Buffy, Willow, and Xander's looks) "Pardon me for finding the glass half full."

—Giles, "The Witch"

"A vampire isn't a person at all. It may have the movements, the memories, even the personality of the person it takes over, but it is a demon at the core. There's no halfway."

—Giles, "Angel"

"I'm not okay. I can't imagine what it's like to be okay. I knew those guys. I go to that room every day. And when I walked in there, it was . . . it wasn't our world anymore. They made it theirs. And they had **fun**."

—Willow, "Prophecy Girl"

Jenny: "How big is a Hellmouth, anyway?"
Giles: "I don't know. Hellmouth-sized."

—"Prophecy Girl"

Willow: "The Lonely Ones?"

Angel: "Vampires."

Xander: "Oh. We usually call them the nasty, pointy, bite-y ones."

Chantarelle: "So many people have that misconception. But they who walk with the night are not interested in harming anyone. They're separate from humanity, and must carry the burden of immortality. They are creatures above us. Exalted."

Angel: "You're a fool."

—"Lie to Me"

"News flash, brain trust. You die. And a demon sets up shop in your old house. It walks and talks and remembers your life, but it's not you."

—Buffy explains the nuances of being sired, "Lie to Me"

"Demons: not that bright."

—Buffy, "Anne"

"Generally speaking? When the scary things get scared? Not good."

—Xander, "Dead Man's Party"

"There's a big evil brewing—you'll never be bored here, Faith, 'cause this is Sunnydale, home of the big brewing evil."

—Willow, "Faith, Hope & Trick"

Giles: "There's a fringe theory held by a few folklorists that some regional stories have actual, very literal antecedents . . ."

Buffy: "And in some language that's English?"

Oz: "Fairy tales are real."

Buffy: "It's all falling into place. Of course, that place is nowhere near this place . . ."

Giles: "There are demons that thrive on fostering persecution and hatred among the mortal animals. Not on destroying men, but on watching them destroy each other. They feed us our darkest fear, and turn peaceful communities into vigilantes."

Buffy: "Hansel and Gretel go home and tell on the mean old witch."

Giles: "And she and probably dozens of others are punished by a righteous mob. It's happened throughout history."

—"Gingerbread"

Giles: "The end of the world."

Xander/Willow: "Again?!"

Xander: "It is losing its impact a little."

Giles: "End of the world. Divisions break down, Hell itself flows into our lives like a sea of fire. Loss, tears, and heartrending pain without end for every human man, woman, and child on this Earth. Death ten times over. For each of you and everyone you love."

Xander: "Hmm. Feeling the impact again."

—"Doomed"

Anya: "Well, see, causing pain *sounds* really cool, I know, but it turns out it's really upsetting. It didn't used to be, but now it is."

Willow: "Is it like you're scared of losing that feeling again, and having it be okay to hurt people, and then you're not in charge of the power anymore because it's in charge of you?"

Anya: "Wow, that was really overdramatically stated, but yeah, that's it."

—"Same Time, Same Place"

Anya: "Vengeance . . ."

D'Hoffryn: "But only to those that deserve it."

Anya: "They all deserve it."

D'Hoffryn: "That's where I was going with that, yeah."

—"Selfless"

"Why would a vampire lie about who sired him?
What's that, some kinda status symbol for the undead:
'My sire can beat up your sire'?"

—**Xander, "Sleeper"**

"Buffy. No matter what your friends expect of you,
evil is a part of us. All of us; it's natural. And no one
can stop that. No one can stop nature."

—**Joyce, "Bring on the Night"**

Buffy: "It claimed to be the original evil, the one
that came before everything else."

Anya: "Please. How many times did I hear that
line in my demon days. 'I'm so rotten they
don't even have a name for it. . . . I'm
baddy bad bad bad. Does it make you
horny?' . . . Or terrified. Whatever."

—**"Bring on the Night"**

Willow: "Last time I tried to use magic . . . the First
turned it around on me. Got inside. I felt it.
Surging through me. In every fiber of my
being. Pure, undiluted evil. I could taste it."
(beat)

Kennedy: "How's evil taste?"

Willow: "Kinda chalky."

—**"The Killer in Me"**

SEX and DATING

"When I'm with a boy I like, it's hard for me to say anything cool, or witty, or at all. . . . I can usually make a few vowel sounds, and then I have to go away."

—Willow, "Welcome to the Hellmouth"

"Senior boys are the only way to go. They're just a better class of person. Senior boys have mystery, they have . . . what's the word I'm searching for? Cars."

—Cordelia, "The Harvest"

199

Xander: "People scoff at things like school spirit, but when you see these young women giving their all like this . . ."
(Amber, an attractive, agile girl, her feet on two chairs, slides down into an extra low split.)

Xander: (mesmerized) ". . . Oooh, stretchy. Where was I?"

Willow: "You were pretending that seeing scantily-clad girls in revealing postures was a spiritual experience."

Xander: "What do you mean, pretending?"

—**"The Witch"**

Xander: "The bracelet. [Buffy] was wearing it, right? That's pretty much like we're going out."

Willow: "Except without the hugging or the kissing or her knowing about it."

—**"The Witch"**

Giles: "The She-Mantis assumes the form of a beautiful young woman and lures innocent virgins back to her nest."

Buffy: "Well, Xander's not a . . . I mean, he's probably—"

Willow: "—going to die!"

—**Xander's in trouble, "Teacher's Pet"**

"I don't think it's bad at all. I think it's really—
(Xander brandishes Buffy's machete, Willow takes a
big step back)—sweet. But certainly nothing I'll ever
bring up again."
    —Willow, re: Xander's virginity, "Teacher's Pet"

"So, how'd the slaying go last night? I mean. . . ." (louder)
"How'd the **laying** go last—no, I don't mean that either."
    —Xander, being subtle,
    "Never Kill a Boy on the First Date"

Giles: "Very well. Follow your hormones. But I
needn't warn you about the hazards of
becoming personally involved with someone
who is unaware of your unique condition."
Buffy: "Yeah, yeah. I've read the back of the box."
Giles: "If your identity as the Slayer is revealed, it
could put you and those around you in
grave danger."
Buffy: "Oh, then in that case I won't wear my button
that says, 'I'm a Slayer—Ask Me How!'"
    —"Never Kill a Boy on the First Date"

Buffy: "What was I supposed to do? Say to Owen,
'Sorry I'm late. I was sitting in a cemetary
with the librarian waiting for a vampire to
rise so that I could prevent an evil prophecy
from coming to pass?"
Xander: (weighing with his hands) "Or . . . flat tire."
    —"Never Kill a Boy on the First Date"

Buffy: (uncapping two lipsticks) "Which one do you think Owen will like better?"

Xander: "Oh, you mean for kissing you and then telling his friends how easy you are so that the whole school loses respect for you and talks behind your back? The red's good."

> —**"Never Kill a Boy on the First Date"**

"You brought a date? Buffy, when I said you could slay vampires and have a social life I didn't mean at the same time!"

> —**Giles, re: finding Owen at the funeral home, "Never Kill a Boy on the First Date"**

Willow: "Omigod—what happened?"

Buffy: "I hit [Xander]. He was trying his hand at felony sexual assault."

Willow: "Oh, Buffy, the hyena in him didn't—"

Buffy: "No, but it's safe to say that in his animal state, his idea of wooing somebody doesn't include a Yanni CD and a bottle of Chianti."

> —**Xander acts on animal instincts, "The Pack"**

"You've been seeing a guy and you don't know what he looks like. Okay, it's a puzzle. No wait, I'm good at these. Does it involve a midget and a block of ice?"

> —**Buffy, on Willow's new boyfriend, "I Robot, you Jane"**

Willow: "When Buffy was a vampire, you weren't still, like, attracted to her, were you?"

Xander: "Willow. How can you—I mean that's really bent, she was grotesque."

Willow: "Still dug her, huh?"

Xander: "I'm sick. I need help."

—**"Nightmares"**

Giles: "And how was your summer?"

Jenny: "Extreme. I did Burning Man in Black Rock. It's such a great festival—you should have been there. There were drum rituals, naked mud-dances, raves, mobile sculptures, you would have just . . . hated it with a fiery passion."

Giles: "Yes, I can't imagine finding any redeeming—naked?"

Jenny: "You probably spent all summer with your nose in a book."

Giles: "I suppose you'd consider that terribly dull."

Jenny: (flirtatiously) "Depends on the book."

—**"When She Was Bad"**

Willow: "Angel came by? Wow. Was there, I mean, was it having to do with kissing?"

Buffy: "Willow, grow up. Not everything is about kissing."

Xander: "Yeah! Some stuff is about groping."

—**"When She Was Bad"**

Angel: "What are you afraid of? Me? Us?"

Buffy: "Uh, could you contemplate getting over yourself? There's no 'us.' I'm sorry if I was supposed to spend the summer mooning over you, but I didn't. I moved on. To the living."

—**"When She Was Bad"**

Buffy: "Are you jealous?"

Angel: "Of Xander? Please. He's just a kid."

Buffy: "Is it 'cause I danced with him?"

Angel: "'Danced with' is a pretty loose term. 'Mated with' might be a little closer—

Buffy: "Oh, you're shocking! One little dance, and you know I just did it to make you crazy, which, by the way, behold my success!"

—**Love makes you do the wacky,**
"Some Assembly Required"

Buffy: "I'd avoid words like 'amenable' and 'indecorous.' Speak English. Just say, 'Hey, I got a thing, you're maybe feeling a thing, and there could be a thing.'"

Giles: "Well, thank you, Cyrano."

—**Dating advice, "Some Assembly Required"**

Buffy: "I'm brainsick. I can't have a relationship with [Angel]."

Willow: "Well, maybe not in the daytime . . . but you could ask him for coffee some night. It's the non-relationship drink of choice. It's not a date, it's a caffeinated beverage— okay, it's hot and bitter, like a relationship in that way, but . . ."

—**"Reptile Boy"**

Angel: "I thought we had . . . you know."

Buffy: "A date? So did I. But who am I kidding? Dates are things normal girls have. Girls who have time to think about nail polish and facials and stuff. You know what I think about? Ambush tactics. Beheading. Not exactly the stuff dreams are made of."

—**"Halloween"**

"Spike is going down. You can attack me, you can send assassins after me . . . that's just fine. But nobody messes with my boyfriend."

—**Buffy, "What's My Line? Part Two"**

Xander: "Are you saying you can't *look* at me when we . . . whatever we do?"

Cordelia: "It's not that I can't. It's more that I . . . don't want to."

—**"Bad Eggs"**

205

"How many of us have lost countless productive hours plagued by unwanted sexual thoughts and feelings?" (Xander's hand shoots up.)

"That was a rhetorical question, Mr. Harris. Not a poll."

—Mr. Whitmore, "Bad Eggs"

Xander: "This thing. With us? Despite our better judgment—it keeps happening. Maybe we should just admit that we're dating—"

Cordelia: "Groping in a broom closet is not dating. You don't call it a date until the guy spends money."

Xander: "Fine. I'll spend—then we'll grope. Whatever. It's just some kind of whacked that we feel we have to hide from all our friends—"

Cordelia: "Well, of course you want to tell everybody. You have nothing to be ashamed of. I, on the other hand, have *everything* to be ashamed of—"

Xander: "Know what? 'Nuff said. Forget it. Must have been my multiple personality guy talking. I call him Idiot Jed, Glutton for Punishment."

—"Surprise"

Cordelia: "So looking at guns makes guys want to have sex? That's scary."

Xander: "Yeah, I guess. . . .

Cordelia: "Well, does looking at guns make **you** wanna have sex?"

Xander: "I'm seventeen. Looking at **linoleum** makes me wanna have sex."

—**"Innocence"**

Buffy: "He'll come around. What guy could resist your wily, Willow charms?"

Willow: "At last count? All of them. Maybe more."

—**"Phases"**

Larry: "Man, Oz, I would love to get me some of that Buffy and Willow action, if you know what I mean."

Oz: "Good job, Larry. You've really mastered the single entendre."

—**"Phases"**

Cordelia: "Sorry, we haven't all perfected that phony 'girl next door' bit."

Willow: "You could be the girl next door too. If Xander lived next to a brothel!"

—**"Phases"**

Xander: "Well, good morning, ladies. And what did you two do last night?"

Willow: "Oh, we had kind of a pyjama-party-sleepover-with-weapons thing."

Xander: "Ah, and I don't suppose either of you had the presence of mind to locate a camera to capture the moment?"

—**"Passion"**

"[Xander] didn't meet anybody over the summer, did he? No, this is Sunnydale, who could he meet except for monsters and stuff; then again he's always kind of attracted to monsters. . . . How's my hair?"

—**Cordelia, "Anne"**

Cordelia: "What is it with you and slayers? Maybe I should dress up like one and hold a stake to your throat."

Xander: "Please, God, don't let that be sarcasm."

—**"Faith, Hope & Trick"**

Xander: "I can handle the Oz full monty."

Willow: "It's not you I'm worried about. It's me. I'm still getting used to half a monty."

Xander: "Half? You and Oz? Which half?"

—**"Beauty and the Beasts"**

"All men are beasts, Buffy. Every guy—from 'Manimal' right on down to 'Mr. I Loved *The English Patient*'—has beast in him. And I don't care how sensitive they act, they're still just in it for the chase. . . ."
—**Faith, "Beauty and the Beasts"**

"Excuse me. When your last steady kills half the class, and then your rebound guy sends you a dump-o-gram? It makes a girl shy."
—**Cordelia, re: Buffy's imaginary secret boyfriend, "Revelations"**

Faith: "Ronnie. Deadbeat. Steve. Klepto. Kenny. DRUMMER. Eventually I had to face up to my destiny as a loser magnet. Now it's strictly get some and get gone. You can't trust guys."

Buffy: "You can trust some guys. Really. I've read about them."
—**"Revelations"**

Faith: "Relax. And take off your pants."
Xander: "Those two concepts are antithetical."
—**"The Zeppo"**

Xander: "[Faith] was fighting one of those apocalypse demon things and I helped her. Gave her a ride home."

Buffy: "And you guys talked?"

Xander: "Not extensively."

Buffy: "Well then why do you—Oh."

Giles: "Ohh."

Willow: "I don't need to say 'oh.' I got it before. They slept together."

—"Consequences"

Buffy: "It was you, Willow, in every detail. Except for your not being a dominatrix . . . as far as we know."

Willow: "Oh, right. Me and Oz play Mistress of Pain every night. Please."

—Did anyone else just go to a scary visual place?, "Doppelgangland"

Anya: "You find me attractive. I've seen you looking at my breasts."

Xander: "Nothing personal. When a guy does that, it just means his eyes are open."

—"Choices"

Willow: "I feel different. You know? I guess that makes sense. Do you feel different? Oh, no, you've already—you probably, not a big change for you, but it's nice—was it nice? Should this be a quiet moment?"

Oz: "I know exactly what you mean."

—Afterglow, "Graduation Day, Part One"

Giles: "I'm not supposed to have a private life?"

Buffy: "No, because you're very, very old, and it's gross."

—"The Freshman"

Oz: "You guys ready to load up and go?"

Willow: "Almost. Buffy's looking at Parker. Who, it turns out, has a reflection, so, big plus there."

—"The Harsh Light of Day"

Parker: "You think I could get a dance with the prettiest girl at the party?"

Buffy: "And what do I do? Stand here and watch?"

—Modest, "The Harsh Light of Day"

Anya: "I can't stop thinking about you. In my dreams sometimes you're all naked."

Xander: "Really? You know, if I'm in the checkout line at Wal-Mart, I've had that same one."

—"The Harsh Light of Day"

Anya: "I have condoms. Some are black."

Xander: "That's very considerate."

Anya: "Please remove your clothing now."

Xander: "And the amazing thing? Still more romantic than Faith."

—**"The Harsh Light of Day"**

Buffy: "So what I'm wondering is, does this always happen? Sleep with a guy and he goes all evil?"

Willow: "Well, from what I understand, pretty much."

—**"The Harsh Light of Day"**

Buffy: "Parker said it's okay to make mistakes. It was sweet."

Willow: "No it wasn't. He said that so you'd take a chance and sleep with him. He's a poop-head."

Buffy: "I know. He's manipulative and shallow and why doesn't he want me? If there was something totally repulsive about me, you'd tell me right?"

Willow: "I'm your friend. I'd call you repulsive in a second."

Buffy: "Maybe me and Parker could still work it out. Do you think we could still work it out?"

Willow: "You're missing something about the whole poop-head principle."

—**"The Harsh Light of Day"**

Willow: "There are other men—better men—men wherein the mind is stronger than the penis."

Xander: "Nothing can defeat the penis!"

—Life after Parker, "Beer Bad"

Willow: "What if the girl wants to and the guy doesn't? That's a bad sign, right?"

Xander: "Could be. Or the girl caught the guy in the one of the seven annual minutes when he's legitimately too preoccupied to do it."

—"Wild at Heart"

"Talk. Keep eye contact. Funny is good, but don't be glib. Remember: If you hurt her, I will beat you to death with a shovel. . . . A vague disclaimer is nobody's friend. Have fun!"

—Willow's advice to Riley on wooing Buffy, "The Initiative"

Xander: "You should go. You could catch it."

Anya: "Then we'll die together! It's romantic. Help me get your trousers off."

Xander: "You're a strange girlfriend."

Anya: "I'm a girlfriend?"

Xander: "Um . . . there's a chance I'm delirious."

Anya: "Ah, yes."

—re: syphilis and company, "Pangs"

Xander: "I think my syphilis is clearing right up."
Anya: "That's nice."
Buffy: "And they say romance is dead."

—**"Pangs"**

"It's just different, you know? A picnic—first of all, daylight, kind of a new venue Buffy-wise . . . and the best part: He said he's bringing all the food. All I have to do is show up and eat—two things I'm really good at!"

—**Buffy, "Something Blue"**

Buffy: "Spike and I are getting married."
Xander: "How? What? How?"
Giles: "Three excellent questions."

—**"Something Blue"**

Xander: "Wish the Buff coulda made it."
Willow: "Guess she's off with Riley. You know how it is with a spanking new boyfriend."
Anya: "Yes, we've enjoyed spanking."

—**"The I in Team"**

"I've seen thousands of relationships. First there's the love and sex. Then there's nothing left but the vengeance. That's how it works."

—**Anya, "Where the Wild Things Are"**

Xander: (to Willow) "So, whatchya been doing? Doing spells?" (to Oz) "She does spells with Tara."

Oz: "I heard about that" (Willow rushes away)

Xander: (sheepish) "Sometimes I think about two women doing a spell . . . and then I do a spell by myself."

—**"Restless"**

"But what else could I expect from a bunch of low-rent, no-account hoodlums like you—hoodlums! Yes. I mean you and your friends, your whole sex; throw 'em all in the sea for all I care, throw 'em in and wait for the bubbles. Men, with your groping and spitting, all groin, no brain, three billion of ya passin' around the same worn-out urge. Men. With your . . . **sales**."

—**Buffy, "Restless"**

Anya: "Maybe we shouldn't do this reintegration thing right away. See, I could take the boys home, have sex with all of us, then we could just slap 'em back together in the morning."

Xander-Double: (smoothly) "She's joking."

Xander: "No, she's *not*! She entirely wants to have sex with us together! It's wrong, and, and . . . it would be very confusing!"

—**Anya wants to double her fun, "The Replacement"**

Nigel:	"I'd like to know a little bit more about the Slayer and about both of you. Your relationship, whatever you can tell me."
Tara:	"Our relationship?"
Willow:	"We're . . . friends."
Tara:	"Good friends."
Willow:	"Girlfriends, actually."
Tara:	"Yes. We're girlfriends."
Willow:	"We're in love. Lovers. We're gay lesbian-type lovers."
Nigel:	"I meant your relationship with the Slayer."
Tara:	"Um . . . just good friends."

—"Checkpoint"

| **Buffy:** | "Maybe it's time for a new tradition: birthdays without boyfriends. It can be just as fun." |
| **Willow:** | "Preaching to the choir here, baby." |

—"Blood Ties"

Buffy:	"What is *this*? The late-night stakeout, the bogus suspects, the flask . . . is this a *date*?"
Spike:	"A—? Please . . . a date? You're completely off your bird. I mean . . . do you want it to be?"
Buffy:	"Oh no. No. . . . Are you out of your mind?"
Spike:	"It's not so unusual. Two people. In the workplace . . . feelings develop."

—"Crush"

Buffy: "I should tell you, I've got this kind of bad history. Where we have coffee and, well, it ends up with you leaving town, and you just got here and everything—"

Ben: "Hmm. Apparently we'd be risking a tragic chain reaction, but I just really like . . . coffee. I think coffee might be worth it. I'd like to get to know coffee better."

—**"I Was Made to Love You"**

Dawn: "I think a date should be in a real fancy restaurant, then champagne at a nightclub with a floor show, then ballroom dancing."

Joyce: "Unfortunately, we're not dating in a movie from the thirties."

—**"I Was Made to Love You"**

Joyce: "Gosh, I'd forgotten how much fun dating can be!"

Buffy: "I don't know, I was standing right there. I didn't see Prince Charming. I didn't see a good night kiss. It all looked pretty tame to me.

Joyce: "Yes, I suppose by your standards it would seem pretty—oh, dear."

Buffy: "What?"

Joyce: "I left my bra in his car."

—**"I Was Made to Love You"**

Anya: "Well, I just feel like I understand sex more. It isn't just about two bodies smooshing together. It's about life."

Xander: "Got it. What makes you feel more alive than the good stuff?"

Anya: "Exactly. Sex is like a party for our aliveness. But it's more than that. It's about *making* life."

—**"Forever"**

Willow: "I think maybe, with your mom and everything, everyone was being all sympathetic, making you feel weak. But Spike wasn't like that. So, just one time, you kind of did something crazy—"

Buffybot: "It wasn't one time. It was lots of times. And lots of different ways. I could make sketches."

—**"Intervention"**

Xander: "It's not a setup."

Anya: "Right, no. It's just an attractive, single man with whom we hope you'll find much in common. . . . And if you happen to forge a romantic relationship leading to babies and many double dates with us so we have someone else to talk to, yay!"

—**"Older and Far Away"**

"Hi, um . . . Tara. How are you? I was wondering . . .
do you want to go out sometime? For coffee? Or
food? Or kisses and gay love?"

—**Willow, "Normal Again"**

Buffy: "I have a date. It's Principal Wood and I
think he's aligned with the First."

Xander: "Also, like, ten years older than you, right?"

Willow: "Which makes him, like, a hundred years
younger than your 'type.'"

Buffy: "Yay, someone who doesn't remember the
industrial revolution."

Willow: "I think they're gonna end up making out.
'Oh, Principal Wood,' she'll gasp, 'I love
your lack of wicked energy. . . .'"

—**"First Date"**

Angel: "I'm gettin' the brush-off for Captain
Peroxide; it doesn't bring out the champion
in me."

Buffy: "Why are you so—are you gonna come by
and get all Dawson on me every time I have
a boyfriend?"

Angel: "Aha! Boyfriend! That'll end well."

Buffy: "And what was the highlight of **our**
relationship? The time you broke up with
me or the time I killed you?"

—**"Chosen"**

Buffy: "I'm cookie dough, okay? I'm not done baking yet. I'm not finished becoming . . . whoever the hell it is I'm going to turn out to be. I've been looking for someone to make me feel whole, and maybe I just need to **be** whole. I make it through this, and the next . . . maybe one day I turn around and realize I'm ready. I'm cookies. And then if I want someone to eat m— or, to enjoy warm delicious cookie-me, then that's fine. That'll be then. When I'm done."

Angel: "Any thoughts on who might enjoy . . . do I have to go with the cookie analogy?"

Buffy: "I don't really think that far ahead. That's kind of the point."

Angel: "I get it."

(A beat, he starts off)

Buffy: "Angel. I do. Sometimes . . . think that far ahead. We both have our lives, but . . . sometimes . . ."

Angel: "Sometimes is something."

—"Chosen"

FRIENDSHIP

Richard: "You have weird friends."
Xander: "News from the file marked 'duh.'"
> **—"Older and Far Away"**

Willow: "Just so you know, I am prepared to hate this woman any way you want."
Buffy: "Will. Thanks, but, no. I don't want to get all, you know, petty."
Willow: "That's the beauty. You can't—I can. Please. Let me carry the hate for both of us."
> **—On the new Mrs. Riley, "As You Were"**

Xander: "I don't know what I'd do . . . without you and Will."
Buffy: "Let's not find out."
> **—"Seeing Red"**

"I'm not protecting you, Jonathan. None of us are. We're doing this for Willow. And the only reason it happens to be your lucky day is because if she kills you, a line gets crossed, I lose a friend. And I hate losing."

—Buffy, "Two to Go"

Willow: "You can't stop this."

Xander: "Yeah, I get that. It's just . . . where else am I going to go? You've been my best friend my whole life. World's gonna end—where else would I want to be?"

—"Grave"

"First day of kindergarten you cried 'cause you broke the yellow crayon and you were too afraid to tell anyone. You've come pretty far; ending the world, not a *terrific* notion, but the thing is, yeah, I love you. I loved crayon-breaking Willow, and I love scary, veiny Willow. So if I'm going out, it's here. You wanna kill the world, you start with me. I've earned that."

—Xander, "Grave"

FUN

Buffy: "So, you like to party with the students? Isn't that kind of skanky?"

Giles: (witheringly) "Right. This is me having fun. I'd much prefer to be home with a cup of Bovril and a good book."

Buffy: "You need a personality, **STAT**."

—**"Welcome to the Hellmouth"**

Cordelia: "Hey, Owen, a bunch of us are loitering at the Bronze tonight. You there?"

Owen: "Tonight? Ooh, we've got the English Lit exam tomorrow. I guess I can get up early. Who's all going?"

Cordelia: (genuinely confused) "You mean besides me?"

Owen: "Buffy, what about you?"

Cordelia: "No, she doesn't—like—fun."

—**"Never Kill a Boy on the First Date"**

"Oh boy, time for geometry." (off Xander and Buffy's looks) "It's fun if you make it fun."

—Willow, "Angel"

"Sure, we saved the world. I say we party. I mean, I got all pretty. . . ."

—Buffy, "Prophecy Girl"

Xander: "So, are we bronzing tonight?"
Willow: "Wednesdays it's kind of beat."
Xander: "Well, we could grind our enemies into talcum powder with a sledgehammer, but, gosh, we did that **last** night."

—"When She Was Bad"

"Darn, I have cheerleader practice tonight. Boy, I wish I'd known you were gonna be digging up dead people **sooner**; I would have cancelled."

—Cordelia, "Some Assembly Required"

"Who needs a social life when they've got their very own Hellmouth?"

—Buffy, "Reptile Boy"

Cordelia: "This isn't about fun tonight, it's about duty: You're here to help me achieve permanent prosperity. Okay, dos and don'ts: Don't wear black, silk, chiffon, or spandex—these are my trademarks—don't do that weird thing to your hair . . ."

Buffy: "What weird—?"

Cordelia: "Don't interrupt. Do be interested if someone should speak to you—may or may not happen—do be polite, do laugh at appropriate intervals—ha ha ha ha—and do lie to your mother about where we're going." (She studies Buffy, tapping her fingers, thinking hard) "Makeup, makeup . . . well, just give it your all and keep to the shadows. We are going to have a blast!"

—**"Reptile Boy"**

Giles: "Yes, even I realize a young person like yourself can't spend all her time fighting the forces of darkness. No slaying this evening. Perhaps you can concentrate on your homework instead."

Buffy: "Do they know about 'fun' in England?"

Giles: "Yes, but it's considered in very poor taste to have any."

—**"Lie to Me"**

"I always say: A day without an autopsy is like a day without sunshine. . . ."

—**Buffy, "Bad Eggs"**

Oz: "So, do you guys steal weapons from the army a lot?"

Willow: "Well, we don't have cable, so we have to make our own fun."

—**"Innocence"**

Oz: "What kind of a deal is this? Is it a gathering, a shindig, or a hootenanny?"

Cordelia: "What's the difference?"

Oz: "A gathering: brie and mellow song stylings. Shindig: dip—*less* mellow song stylings. Perhaps a large amount of malt beverage. And a hootenanny . . . just chock full of hoot and a little bit of nanny."

—**"Dead Man's Party"**

"I know you all think it's just a big, dumb, girly thing, but it's not. Some of the skaters are Olympic medal winners, and my dad buys me cotton candy, a different stuffed animal wearing fuzzy skates every year, and okay it *is* a big, dumb, girly thing, but I love it."

—**Buffy thinks Brian Boitano doing "Carmen" is a life-changer, "Helpless"**

Angel: "The prom?"

Buffy: "Yeah. You know, the big 'end-of-high-school-right-of-passage' thingy . . . ? Imagine a cotillion with spiked punch and the electric slide."

—**"Choices"**

Oz: "Once again, the Hellmouth puts the 'special' in special occasion."

Xander: "Why do I even buy tickets for these things? I ask you."

Willow: "I wonder if I can take my dress back."

Buffy: "Don't you dare. . . . You guys are gonna have a prom. The kind of prom everyone should have. I will give you all a nice, fun, normal evening . . . if I have to kill every single person on the face of the Earth to do it."

Xander: "Yay?"

—**"Choices"**

"I've got two words that are going to take all the pain away: Miniature. Golf."

—**The Mayor, "Enemies"**

Riley: "So what have you got going on tonight?"
Buffy: "Patrolling."
Riley: "Patrolling?"
Buffy: "Petroleum."
Riley: "Petroleum."
Buffy: "Uh-huh."
Riley: "Tonight you have crude oil."
Buffy: "And homework. What about you?"
Riley: "Oh, you know, grading papers."
Buffy: "Well, that'll be fun."
Riley: "Not petroleum fun, but it passes the time."
　　　—Secret identities are a nuisance, "Hush"

"I was kind of unsure about where the party was. And then I saw the flashing red lights and the ambulance, and it's like, oh right, of course. Carnage. Death. It's a Buffy party."

—Buffy, "Doomed"

"You know, it's nice having everyone together for my birthday. Of course, you could smash all my toes with a hammer and it would still be the bestest Buffy birthday ever."

—Buffy, "A New Man"

Buffy: "Faith is back, and like it or not, she's my responsibility."
Willow: "Yeah, too bad. That was the funnest coma ever."

—"This Year's Girl"

Anya: "Come share in the joy of our groove
thang."

Willow: "And despite that, I succumb to the beat."

Buffy: "I'll catch the next Soul Train out."

—"Dead Things"

"So, you ever think about, maybe, not celebrating
your birthday? Just to try it, I mean."

—Spike, to Buffy, "Older and Far Away"

DEATH

Buffy: "My philosophy is 'life is short.' Not original, I'll grant you. But it's true. Seize the moment. 'Cause tomorrow you might be dead."

Willow: "Oh . . . that's nice . . ."

—**"Welcome to the Hellmouth"**

"I'm reading about death all the time, and I've never seen a dead body before. Do they usually move?"

—**Owen confronts un-death,
"Never Kill a Boy on the First Date"**

"I don't understand how this all happens, how we go through this. I mean, I know [Joyce], and then she's . . . there's just a body; I don't under stand why she just can't get back in it and not be dead. It's stupid, it's mortal and stupid. Xander's crying and not talking and I was having fruit punch and I thought that Joyce would never have any more fruit punch and she'd never have eggs, or yawn, or brush her hair, not ever and no one will explain. . . ."

—**Anya, "The Body"**

Dawn: "So, what? Life just goes on and I forget Mom? Is that what you're saying?

Willow: "Not forget. No. You . . ."

Tara: "You make a place in your heart for her. It's sort of like she becomes part of you. In the things she showed you and taught you . . . the way you live your life."

—"Forever"

"Every day you wake up it's the same bloody question that haunts you: Is today the day I die? It's a warrior's pain, a warrior's question, and you ask it every time the sun rises. And every day you manage to survive, you're only partly relieved because you know—it's just a matter of time. Death is on your heels, baby— and, sooner or later, it's going to catch you. . . . And some part of you *wants* it. Not only to stop the fear and the uncertainty, but because you're a little bit in love with it. Death is your art. You make it with your hands, day after day. Part of you is desperate to know . . . what's it like? That's also a warrior's question. A warrior's curiosity. . . . So you see, that's the secret. Not the punch she didn't throw or the kick she didn't land. She simply wanted it. Every Slayer has a death wish."

—Spike, "Fool for Love"

Primitive: "Death is your gift."

Buffy: "Okay. No. Death is not a gift. My mother just died and I know about this. It's not a gift I want and it's not a gift I want to give to anyone else. If I have to kill demons because it helps the world, then I kill demons, but it's not a *gift* to anybody."

—**"Intervention"**

Spike: "Well, I haven't been to a Hell-dimension just of late, but I know a thing or two about torment—"

Buffy: "I was happy. Wherever I . . . was . . . I was happy. At peace. I knew that everyone I cared about was all right. I *knew* it. Time didn't mean anything, nothing had form . . . but it was still *me*, you know? And I was warm and I was loved . . . and I was finished. Complete. I don't understand about dimensions or theology or any of . . . but I think I was in heaven. And now I'm not. I was torn out of there. My friends pulled me out. And everything here is bright and hard and violent. . . . Everything I feel, everything I touch . . . this is Hell."

—**"After Life"**

"You're trying to sell me on the world. The one where you lie to your friends when you're not trying to kill them, and you screw a vampire just to feel, and insane asylums are the comfy alternative. This world? Buffy, it's me. I know you were happier in the ground, hanging with the worms. The only time you were ever at peace in your whole life is when you were dead. . . ."

—Willow, "Two to Go"

Buffy: "I'm trying to protect you."

Dawn: "Well, you can't! Look around, Buffy. We're trapped in here! Willow's killing and people I love keep dying and you *cannot protect me from that*!"

—"Grave"

LOVE

"Angel. Yeah, I can see him in a
relationship. 'Hi, honey, you're in
grave danger, see you next
month.'"

—Buffy, "Angel"

"Guys'll do anything to impress a girl. I once drank an entire gallon of Gatorade without taking a breath."

—Xander, "Angel"

"A vampire in love with the Slayer. It's rather poetic, in a maudlin sort of way."

—Giles, on Angel, "Out of Mind, Out of Sight"

"Love makes you do the wacky."

—Willow, "Some Assembly Required"

Buffy: "I don't get it. Why would anyone want to *make* a girl?"

Xander: "You mean when there's so many pre-made ones just lying around?" (shrugs) "The things we do for love. I'll tell you this. People don't fall in love with what's right in front of them. People want the dream. What they can't have. The more unattainable, the more attractive."

Buffy: "But it's not . . . doable, is it? I mean, making someone from scraps? Actually making them live?"

Willow: "If it is, my science project's definitely coming in second this year."

Xander: "And speaking of love . . ."

Willow: "We were talking about the reanimation of dead tissue."

Xander: "Do I deconstruct your segues? Yeesh."

—"Some Assembly Required"

Xander: "Well, I guess that makes it official. Everyone's paired off. Vampires can get dates. Hell, even the school librarian is seeing more action than me." (shakes his head) "You ever feel like the world is a game of musical chairs, and the music has stopped and you're the only one who doesn't have a chair?"

(Cordelia steps up behind Willow and Xander, summons her nerve.)

Willow: "All the time."

Cordelia: "Xander, I, uh, just wanted to say thanks for saving my life in there. It was . . . really brave and heroic and all. And if there's ever anything I can do to repay you . . ."

Xander: "Do you mind? We're talking here." (Cordelia reacts, turns, and crosses off)

Xander: (to Willow) "So, where were we?"

Willow: "Wondering why we never seem to have dates."

Xander: "Oh, yeah. So, why do you think that is?"

—**"Some Assembly Required"**

Xander: "It's sad. Granted. But let's look at the upside for a moment. I mean, what kind of future could she have really had with him? Working two jobs. Denny's waitress by day, Slayer by night. Angel's always in front of the tube, with a big ol' blood belly . . . and he's dreaming of the glory days when Buffy still thought the whole creature of the night routine was a big turn-on . . ."

Willow: "You've thought way too much about this—"

Xander: "That's just the beginning. You want to hear the part where I fly into town in my private jet and take Buffy out for prime rib?"

—**"Surprise"**

Cordelia: "You were too busy rushing off to die for your beloved Buffy. . . . You'd never die for me."

Xander: "I might die *from* you, does that get me any points?"

—**"Innocence"**

"Spike, my boy, you really don't get it. You tried to kill her and you couldn't. Look at you. You're a wreck. She's stronger than any Slayer you've faced. Force won't get it done. You gotta work from the inside. To kill this girl . . . you have to love her."

—**Angel, "Innocence"**

"Sometimes when I'm sitting in class, I'm not thinking about class, 'cause that could never happen, and I'll think about kissing you and then everything stops. It's like, freeze frame. Willow kissage."

—Oz, "Innocence"

Willow: "Right now, Oz and I are in some sort of holding pattern. Only without the holding. Or anything else."

Cordelia: "Well, what's he waiting for? What's his problem . . . ? Oh, that's right. He's a guy."

Willow: "Yeah. Him and Xander. Guys."

Cordelia: "Who do they think they are?"

Willow: "A couple of guys."

—"Phases"

"Well, I like you. You're nice, and you're funny, and you don't smoke, and okay, werewolf, but that's not all the time. I mean, three days out of the month *I'm* not much fun to be around either."

—Willow to Oz, "Phases"

Buffy: "Valentine's Day is just a gimmick to sell cards."

Amy: "Bad breakup?"

Buffy: "Believe me when I say 'Uh huh.'"

—"Bewitched, Bothered, and Bewildered"

"Passion. . . . It is born . . . and though uninvited, unwelcome, unwanted . . . like a cancer, it takes root. It festers. It bleeds. It scabs . . . only to rupture, and bleed anew. It grows . . . it thrives . . . until it consumes. It lives . . . so, it must die . . . in time."

—Angel, "Passion"

Buffy: "It's so weird. . . . Every time something like that happens my first instinct is to run to tell Angel. I can't believe it's the same person. He's the complete opposite of what he was."

Willow: "Well . . . sort of, except . . ."

Buffy: "Except what?"

Willow: "You're still the only thing he thinks about."

—"Passion"

Buffy: "Sometimes I wonder if any good ever comes of it."

Giles: "Comes of what?"

Buffy: "Falling in love. Letting your emotions call the shots for you. Because if there is an upside, I sure haven't come across it."

—"Passion"

"You know, lots of people lose themselves in love. It's no shame. They write songs about it. The hitch is, you can't stay lost. Sooner or later, you have to get back to yourself. If you can't, love becomes your master. And you're just its dog."

—**Mr. Platt, "Beauty and the Beasts"**

Angel: "Am I going to see you this weekend? You probably have plans. . . ."

Buffy: "Birthday, right. Actually, yeah, I do have a thing."

Angel: "A thing? A date?"

Buffy: "Nice attempt at casual. It is a date. Older man. Very handsome. Likes it when I call him 'Daddy.'"

Angel: (smiles) "Your father. . . ." (suddenly worried) "It **is** your father . . . ?"

—**"Helpless"**

Angel: "I watched you, I saw you called. It was a bright afternoon, out in front of your school, you walked down the steps and I loved you."

Buffy: "Why?"

Angel: "Because I could see your heart. You held it before you for everyone to see and I worried that it would be bruised or torn. More than anything in my life I wanted to keep it safe, to warm it with my own."

Buffy: "That's beautiful. . . . Or, taken literally, incredibly gross."

—"Helpless"

Angel: "You still my girl?"

Buffy: "Always."

—"Enemies"

Buffy: "You never take me anyplace new."

Angel: "What about that fire demon nest in the caves near the beach? Thought that was a nice change of pace."

—"Choices"

"When it comes to you, Angel, Buffy's not a Slayer. She's just like any other young woman in love. You're all she can see of tomorrow. But I think we both know there's gonna be some hard choices ahead. If she can't make them, you're going to have to. . . . I know you care about her. I just hope you care enough."

—Joyce, "Choices"

"You deserve more. You deserve something outside of . . . demons and darkness. You should have someone who can take you into the light."

—Angel to Buffy, "Choices"

"Yes, men like sports. Men watch the action movie. They eat of the beef and enjoy to look at the bosoms. A thousand years avenging their wrongs and that's all you learned?"

—Xander to Anya, "Graduation Day, Part One"

Angel: "Are you mad at me for being around too much or for not being around enough?"

Buffy: "Duh—yes."

—"Graduation Day, Part One"

Anya: "When I think something bad might happen to you, it feels bad. Inside. Like I might vomit."

Xander: "Welcome to the world of romance."

Anya: "It's horrible! No wonder I used to get so much work."

—**"Graduation Day, Part One"**

Willow: "So, spill. What was that all about, with the cutie patootie?"

Buffy: "I don't know. Nothing serious, I think. Just random adorableness."

Xander: "A technique I know well. Hit the girl with your best shot, and then—hasta."

Oz: "Gotta respect the drive-by."

—**Hit-and-run Parker, "The Freshman"**

Harmony: "I don't know why I let you be so mean to me."

Spike: "Love hurts, baby."

—**"The Harsh Light of Day"**

"I just kinda feel like there's a pattern here. Open your heart to someone and he . . . he bails on you. Maybe it would be easier to just not let anyone in anymore."

—**Buffy, "Fear, Itself"**

"Love. It's a logic blocker."

—**Xander, "Wild at Heart"**

Buffy: "I've never seen her like this before, Giles. It's like it hurts too much to even form words."

Giles: "But you've felt that way yourself, and you got through it."

Buffy: "Well, I ran away and went to hell—and then I got through it. I'm kind of hoping Willow won't use me as a model."

—**"Wild at Heart"**

Willow: "Oz . . . don't you love me?"

Oz: "My whole life, I've never loved anything else."

—**"Wild at Heart"**

Riley: "I just didn't like hearing him talk that way about Buffy. I think I . . . well, I guess I like her."

Forrest: "You're kind of like a moron."

—**"The Initiative"**

Willow: "Okay. Let's say I help. And you start a
conversation. It goes great. You like Buffy.
She likes you. You spend time together.
Feelings grow deeper, and one day without
even realizing it, you find you're in love.
Time stops and it feels like the whole
world's made for you two alone until the
day one of you leaves and rips the
still-beating heart from the other, who's
now a broken, hollow mockery of the
human condition."

Riley: "Yep. That's the plan."

—**"The Initiative"**

Buffy: "I don't know. I love being around Riley, I
think he cares about me, but . . . I still feel
like something's missing. . . ."

Willow: "He's not making you miserable?"

Buffy: "Exactly!"

—**"Something Blue"**

"I can't help thinking, isn't that where the fire comes
from? Can a nice, safe relationship be that intense?
It's nuts, but part of me believes that real love and
passion *have* to go hand in hand with lots of pain and
fighting."

—**Buffy, "Something Blue"**

"I'm confused. But I can feel my skin humming—my hands, my . . . every inch of me. I've never been this excited by a girl and I'm not trying to scare you, not gonna force myself on you, but I am by God not gonna walk away because I think it might not work."

—Riley, "Doomed"

Riley:	"This you-and-me thing? It's stupid."
Buffy:	"Right. Which is why we can't. Do the you-and-me thing."
Riley:	"No. I mean *you're* stupid. I mean, I don't mean that . . . no, I think maybe I do."
Buffy:	"Wow. Sweet talk like that will melt my reservations."

—"Doomed"

"Welcome to the story of the world! Things fall apart, Buffy. Evil—it comes and goes. But the way people manage is, they don't do it alone. They pull each other through. And, sometimes, they even enjoy themselves."

—Riley, "Doomed"

"To my wife. What would I do without you, beautiful? Well, for starters I probably wouldn't need to drink so much, would I? But on the bright side, being married probably saved me from the clap, so here's to ya."

—Mr. Harris, "Hell's Bells"

Dawn: "I thought [Xander and Anya] were happy."

Buffy: "They were. I know they were. They were my light at the end of the tunnel. . . . I guess they were a train."

—**"Hell's Bells"**

Spike: "I've tried to make it clear to you, but you won't see it. Something happened to me. The way I feel . . . about you . . . it's different. No matter how hard you try to convince yourself it isn't. It's real."

Buffy: "I think it is. . . . For you."

—**"Entropy"**

Woman at bar: "He said he loved me!"

Anya: "Oh, gee, then I guess he must have meant it, 'cause, hey—guys never say anything they don't really mean, do they?"

—**"Seeing Red"**

"Trust is for old marrieds, Buffy. Great love is wild and passionate and dangerous. It burns and consumes."

—**Spike, "Seeing Red"**

Woman: "You're all wet."

Xander: "Good thing I'm part fish."

Woman: "Which part?"

Xander: "The part with the hook in it."

Woman: "Careful. Someone might reel you in."

Xander: "Yeah, but then there'd be the flopping and the gasping, and sure, maybe it'd work out, but chances are I'd up and leave you at the helm in your white dress, and then find you spawning with another fish, who turns out to be spawning my very good friend night and day behind my back, and then comes the fighting, and again the flopping and the gasping, 'cause, hey, chicken of the sea not doing great with the women these days."

—**"Seeing Red"**

Anya: "They say, 'Oh, Anya, I want to be with you for the rest of my life,' and you believe them; you believe they feel the same way you do, because that's the way love's supposed to work, right?"

Woman at bar: "Who's Anya?"

Anya: "Then you get all excited with the tingly anticipation, but wait! Not so fast! There's the apocalypse and the back from the grave and the blah blah blah and by the time you're finally standing in that beautifully expensive white dress you've dreamed of wearing ever since you became human, he's gone all heebie-jeebie and decides he'd rather go steady."

—"Seeing Red"

"See, this is what I hate about you vampires. Sex and death and pain and love: It's all the same damn thing to you."

—Buffy, "Conversations with Dead People"

"I've come to redefine the words 'pain' and 'suffering' since I fell in love with you."

—Spike to Buffy, "Never Leave Me"

Buffy: "I love you."

Spike: "No, you don't. But thanks for saying it."

—"Chosen"

RELIGION

Xander: "You gotta take care of the egg. It's a baby, gotta keep it safe and teach it Christian values."
Willow: "My egg is Jewish."
Xander: "Then teach it that dreidel song."
—"Bad Eggs"

"Ira Rosenberg's only daughter nailing crucifixes to her bedroom wall? I have to go to Xander's house just to watch *A Charlie Brown Christmas* every year."
—Willow, "Passion"

Young Woman: Have you accepted Jesus Christ as your personal savior?"
Buffy: "Well, you know, I meant to, and then I was busy all day. . . ."
—"The Freshman"

"So, um, about being a nun? With the whole abjuring the company of men thing? How's that working for you? The abjuring."
—Buffy, "Triangle"

Tentacle Demon: "So you think the children should
be raised in ignorance of our ways?"

Cousin Carol: "No, no. The Harrises are very
broad-minded. We're Episcopalians."

> **—A beautiful melding of
> two cultures, "Hell's Bells"**

MISCELLANEOUS

"I'm an old-fashioned girl. I was raised to believe the men dig up the corpses and the women have the babies."
—Buffy, "Some Assembly Required"

Willow: "By the way, are we hoping to find a body, or no body?"

Xander: "Call me an optimist, but *I'm* hoping to find a fortune in gold doubloons."
—Xander's got a fresh perspective, "Some Assembly Required"

"A Slayer with family and friends. That sure as hell wasn't in the brochure."
—Spike, "School Hard"

Willow: (to Angel) "Why do you think she went to that party? Because you gave her the brush off . . ." (to Giles) ". . . and you never let her do anything, except work and patrol and—I know she's the Chosen One, but you're killing her with the pressure; she's sixteen going on forty—" (to Angel) "—and you, I mean you're gonna live forever, you don't have time for a cup of coffee?" (takes a breath) "Okay. I don't feel better now and we gotta help Buffy."
—"Reptile Boy"

Buffy:	"Hey! Are you busy tonight?"
Ford:	"I'm hoping you'll tell me I am."
Buffy:	"We're going to the Bronze. It's the local club and you gotta come."
Ford:	"I'd love to, but if you guys had plans— would I be imposing?"
Xander:	"Only in the literal sense."

—**"Lie to Me"**

Willow:	"Why are you so interested in Ford?"
Cordelia:	"In case you haven't noticed, there is a devastating cute guy shortage right now. The government is calling for rationing, so why does [Buffy] get to horde them all? So, come on, what's Ford interested in?"
Willow:	"Vampires."
Cordelia:	(deflated) "Oh, great. That's Buffy's best subject. You sure he doesn't like clothes?"

—**"Lie to Me"**

Buffy:	"People are perfectly happy, getting along, then vampires come in and they run around and they kill people and they make these stupid little pizzas and everyone's like, 'ooh, wow . . .'"
Giles:	"Uh, Buffy, I believe the subtext here is rapidly becoming the text."

—**Re: Ted, "Ted"**

Xander: (doing a little mock-childish dance)
"You've got parental issues, you've got parental issues. Freud would have said the exact same thing. Except he might not have done the little dance."

—Re: Buffy's feelings toward Ted, "Ted"

Willow: "I'm sure it wasn't your fault. He started it!"
Buffy: "Yeah, that defense only works in six-year-old court, Will."

—"Ted"

Giles: "I suppose there is a sort of Machiavellian ingenuity to your transgression."
Xander: "I resent that . . . ! Or, possibly, thank you . . ."
Giles: "Bit of both would suit."

—"Bad Eggs"

Buffy: "Conjuring? Let's be honest, Will. Your basic spells are usually about fifty-fifty."
Willow: "Oh, yeah?! Well . . . so's your face!"

—"Fear, Itself"

Spike: "I don't understand. This sort of thing's never happened to me before."

Willow: "Maybe you were nervous."

Spike: "I felt all right when we started. . . ."

Willow: "You're probably just trying too hard. Doesn't this happen to every vampire?"

Spike: "Not to me, it doesn't!"

Willow: "It's me, isn't it?"

Spike: "What are you talking about?"

Willow: "You came looking for Buffy, then settled. You didn't want to bite me. I just happened to be around."

Spike: "Piffle!"

Willow: "I know I'm not the kind of girl vamps want to sink their teeth into. It's always, 'You're like a sister to me,' or 'Oh, you're such a good friend.'"

Spike: "Don't be ridiculous. Why, I'd bite you in a heartbeat."

Willow: "Really?"

Spike: "Thought about it."

Willow: "When?"

Spike: "Remember last year? You had on that fuzzy pink number with the lilac underneath. . . ."

Willow: "I never would have guessed. You play the blood-lust kind of cool."

Spike: "I hate being obvious. All fang-y and 'grr.' Takes the mystery out."

—**"The Initiative"**

Tara: "I was just afraid if you saw the kind of people I came from . . . you wouldn't wanna be anywhere near me."

Willow: "See? That's where you're a dummy. I think about what you grew up with, and then look at what you are . . . it makes me proud. It makes me love you more."

Tara: "Every time I . . . even at my worst, you always make me feel special. How do you do that?"

Willow: "Magic."

—"Family"

"We find the nest—as in now—or Sunnydale turns into the TROUBLEmeat Palace. . . . I wish I'd said something else."

—Buffy, "As You Were"

"ONCE MORE, WITH FEELING"

Buffy: "I'm just worried this whole session is going to turn into a training montage from an eighties movie."

Giles: "Well, if we hear any inspirational power chords, we'll just lie down until they go away."

"I'm pretty spry for a corpse."

—Buffy

Henchman: "My master has the Slayer's sister hostage at the Bronze because she summoned him and at midnight he's gonna take her to the underworld to be his queen."

Giles: "What does he want?"

Henchman: (pointing to Buffy) "Her. Plus chaos and insanity and people burning up, but that's more big-picture stuff."

"So Dawn's in trouble. It must be Tuesday."

—Buffy

"I've seen some of these underworld child-bride deals and they never end well. Maybe once."

—Anya

"The hardest thing in this world is to live in it."

—Dawn

"CHOSEN"

Willow: "The First is scrunched, so . . . what do you think we should do, Buffy?"

Faith: "Yeah, you're not the one and only Chosen anymore. Just gotta live like a person. How's that feel?"

Dawn: "Buffy? What **are** we gonna do now?" (Buffy looks at them, looks back at the crater, and we are in full close-up as she considers the question, a small smile creeping onto her lips as she decides on her answer.) Black Out.

End of Show